Grumble Fast

40-Day Gratitude Feast

Teaching Devotional

RUTH WEBB

Published by Heart of the Psalmist Inc
P.O. Box 133 Eaglehawk, Vic, 3556

Prophetic Artwork by Susie Ruehlemann – ariseartproject.com
Mountain of the Lord – Watch - Lion of Judah

The gold stopwatch set to 40 represents the importance of 40 days (p.18 'Why Grumble Fast'). The Lion of Judah is roaring over us. Golden floating musical notes represent the glory, high praises, new sounds, and victorious worship warfare. Purple tones represent royalty of the King of kings and His Mount Zion on which the Tabernacle of David was pitched —the worship and governmental capital of Israel and the resting place of the presence of God.

Editor: Carol Martinez

ISBN: 978-0-9587437-3-0

Warranty: If instructions are followed closely, you
will enter through the gates of praise.

Warning: This book is a danger to the habit of grumbling.

Endorsements

Grumble Fast: 40-Day Gratitude Feast is a must-read attitude changer. Written with great insight from passages in the Bible, Ruth Webb applies principles that will lead to heart change; and as a result, changes in our lives. After all, what we say and do is really a reflection of what is in our heart. This is not only a must-read, but a good reference to have at our bedside tables to disciple us through those attitude challenges in our life. This is a book you enter one way, and after reading it, leave a different way.

Susan Rowe
Co-founder, The Global Watch
www.theglobalwatch.com

Grumble Fast: 40-Day Gratitude Feast by Ruth Webb has the potential to help people break through their obstacles and snap the chains that hold them back. As Ruth says in her book, 'Praise is a potent weapon against the devil—somewhat like a nuclear bomb.' So is gratitude. Words are powerful. Read this book and do the *40-Day Grumble Fast* and you will never be the same again. I encourage you to buy this book and read it!

Warwick Marsh
National Day of Prayer & Fasting, Australia

When we were asked (in 2004), to lead the international prayer and fasting event in Australia known as 'The Call', I began to contact national leaders about joining this significant prayer for Australia. I was surprised when many responded, 'Who prays and fasts anymore?' Obviously they needed to do this *40-Day Grumble Fast* that Ruth Webb has blessed the body of Christ with. Fasting and prayer shifts nations and will shift your life for good. Fasting takes many forms. It starts with us lining up our words with God's words. Step into this *Grumble Fast* and allow God to change your world and those around you in the process.

Bruce Lindley

Apostle ARC Global Apostolic Community
https://www.australianarc.org.au/

Grumble Fast is deeply convicting and is being released at a strategic time in the Kingdom. The prophets have been warning in this Hebraic year 5780, meaning *Pey* (mouth), to remember that life and death are in the power of the tongue. Ruth has expanded on this warning, giving us keys to overcome the temptation to negatively grumble. Each 40-day reading gives Scriptures to meditate upon a short teaching to equip us, activations to empower us, and prayer for strength and guidance. She expounds on how grumbling is the antithesis to thanksgiving. I highly recommend you buy a copy and start your *40-day Grumble Fast.* It will be life changing!

Jenny Hagger AM

Director - Australian House of Prayer for All Nations.
Lead Pastor, Kingsgate Hub
https://www.ahopfan.com

Are you ready for a lifestyle that opens up the gates of Heaven's presence, revelation and favour over your life? In *Grumble Fast*, anointed worship leader Ruth Webb reveals how grumbling opens up the door for enemy activity, whereas gratitude is the key that releases the presence of Heaven.

Grumble Fast not only explains the importance of gratitude, but also takes readers on a practical 40-day journey with the goal of changing our grumbling habits. Each day offers readers fresh inspiration. It is a practical, challenging and insightful book that I heartily recommend.

Enoch Lavender

Pastoral Leader: Shalom Israel, Melbourne
https://shalomisrael.com.au

Wow. This book is amazing. Everyone should read it. Ruth Webb is a good friend who has led worship for our breakthroughs in Jerusalem. What she has written is by inspiration of the Spirit of the Lord. The pages come from the throne of grace. Soldiers of the cross are encouraged to get on that narrow pathway and fight the good fight. The mandate to stop grumbling is a direct order from the Lord to help prepare His bride.

Karen Dunham

Pastor, Living Bread Church International
(USA, Jerusalem, Nairobi)
https://livingbreadchurch.com

Grumble Fast: 40-Day Gratitude Feast speaks of supernatural deliverance, healing, and total freedom. Fasting and prayer are one of the most powerful spiritual combinations on earth. True fasting brings humility, alignment with God, breaks the power of flesh and demons, and brings answers to prayer when nothing else works. Prayer is not preparation for the battle – prayer is the battle. Ruth Webb is living testimony she has learned how to prevail over rejection, depression, and bitterness. This book teaches and encourages men and women to fulfil their potential of God's calling and purpose.

Dr. Daniel Rozen
Senior Pastor and Founder,
Israel Living Stone Ministries
www.livingstoneministriesisrael.com

I highly recommend *Grumble Fast*—it's a Glory Buster! This devotional will help us break out of confined mindsets that have held us hostage, and will, instead, ignite passion and help us step into glory realms! Now is the time to fast and pull down the strong hold of grumbling. In this era of *Pey*, enter through gratitude to hear and embrace fresh creative thoughts of God! If you want to experience more of His glory, then NOW is the time to join Ruth in this transformational tool and see a generation set free from a mindset of grumbling! Let's do it.

Rhona Bailey
Apostle / Prophet for Tehillah Apostolic Network
United Kingdom

This devotional book is a valuable contribution to all believers. Grumbling and complaining is something that we all can do and it hinders the work of God in our lives and ministries. Ruth has done a worthwhile service to the body of Christ by providing a practical resource to help believers break such habits and be full of gratitude and thanksgiving!

Pastor Jamie Pryor
Canberra, Australia

Acknowledgements

I am grateful!

I so appreciate my Heavenly Father's love and acceptance, Yeshua's redemptive sacrifice and Holy Spirit's help. I give thanks for the many precious people You have placed in my life.

- Laurence, my beloved: your love and faithfulness is steadfast and enabling. You are a rare and precious jewel.
- So appreciative of the gift of children and grandchildren. Luke, Rachel and Luke, Isabelle and Imogen: you are treasures; you keep me grounded and fill my arms and heart with love. You and your generations stir my prayer journey.
- The faithful worshippers and intercessors at Tabernacle of David (Bendigo): you are precious friends, brave warriors, and extravagant lovers of God. You embraced the *Grumble Fast* and your feedback and breakthroughs inspired this book. You have bravely joined me as we ventured into unchartered waters in worship and Holy Spirit adventures. Together the Lord has helped us test and refine His (at times scary) new directions. I have valued your prayers, support, suggestions, and courage.
- So grateful for the assistance given in editorial and theological advice (Laurence), Scripture references (Jennifer), and putting together the daily emails for the 40-day fast (Anita).

- I am appreciative of all who wrote kind words of endorsement: I am not just grateful for what you have written, but also for your friendships, encouragement and inspiration along life's journey.
- My gratitude to South Australian prophetic artist Susie Ruehlemann who spent much time in seeking the Lord for His inspired downloads to paint from, and also lovingly and graciously encouraging me and incorporating my insights.
- Special thanks to Anne Hamilton for writing the foreword, and Carol Martinez for her patient editing and layout design.
- And of the many friends with whom we have shared the worship journey through Australia, New Zealand, Asia and Israel: only eternity knows…

Contents

Foreword

Gratitude and grace are companion words—they both spring out of old terms for *favour.*

Grumble and grim are also related! And they're both mired in words for *anger.*

It doesn't take a degree in rocket science to know that, when we show gratitude, we are not only expressing thankfulness for favour but we are also more likely to be favoured in the future. After all, no one likes to see their costly gift shoved aside by some-one with an ungrateful heart.

This devotional is not just about the discipline of not grum-bling, it's also about the blessings that come from an attitude of gratitude. On the one hand, it's preventative; on the other, it's restorative.

As you practise *not* grumbling, as you instead declare your thankfulness and deepen your recognition of God's work in your life, joy will rise. As you praise Him, He will come to inhabit your praises—and show Himself strong on your behalf as Immanuel, *God with us.*

Be blessed as you start your *Grumble Fast.*

Anne Hamilton

Award winning author of over 20 books
Armour Books Series: Strategies for the Threshold #1-4
Armour Books Series: Devotional Theology # 1-5
New Series: Jesus and the Healing of History

Preface

Gratitude is the heart of true worship. As kingdoms clash in these end-times, Holy Spirit is calling us higher in worship, to realms of Throne-room Glory. It is the place we win major battles. But how far worship warriors rise into glory realms will be proportional to their victory over grumbling.

The Lord is urgently speaking to the Body of Christ about what comes out of our mouths. The Hebraic year 5780 began at Feast of Trumpets 2019. The Hebrew name for 80 is *pey*, which means mouth. At the start of a new year and decade, and as the earth becomes more toxic and dark, the Lord is calling His people to loudly proclaim, even roar, His powerful Words and decrees. Simultaneously, He is warning us to conquer our human default and – demonic seduction – to grumble, complain and accuse.

Praise is a potent weapon against the devil—somewhat like a nuclear bomb. In the Army or Air Force, to protect against unwanted damage, stringent training and protocols are in place for those operating lethal weapons. In the kingdom of God, the weapon of praise operates through a susceptible instrument, namely our tongues. James calls it an untameable fire! Because it contains the power of life and death, it is an area of severe warfare and vulnerability. James challenges every worshipper with the need to allow Holy Spirit to train and harness this power. *'If someone believes they have a relationship with God but fails to guard his words then his heart is drifting away and his religion is shallow and empty.'* (James 1:26 TPT)

Drifting hearts? Shallow religion? Ouch. Let me challenge you further with this next question. If gratitude and praise are the language of heaven, where is the language of grumbling spoken?

At four milestones in my life, the Lord challenged me to give thanks. Each time I wrestled, like a great tug-o-war, between grumbling and gratitude! But each time I obeyed and gave thanks, I encountered breakthroughs that impacted destiny. Giving thanks in the midst of chaos is not about being in denial. Rather, it is honestly facing our stuff, yet trusting the Lord to help us, because His ways and thoughts are higher than our devastation!

I discovered three accumulative keys:

1. Thanksgiving must begin in the heart.
2. Thanksgiving is key to true worship.
3. Overcoming destructive demonic plans is dependent on both #1 and #2.

In many circles, people know me as a Throne-Room worship leader. But this was not always the case. Musically and spiritually it has been a lifetime journey.

I began life as a negative person—the glass was mostly half empty! Growing up I was prone to moodiness and anger; I was a loner, and an expert in sarcasm. A heart full of rejection fuelled my sharp tongue. And the devil seemed much more powerful than God! Not a recommended character reference for a potential worship leader!

There are four critical junctures in my story when I was challenged to change my mindset and position my heart for worship. Each time, I've witnessed significant destiny barriers removed.

1. The Charismatic renewal swept the world, my local church and my family in the 1970s. But I resisted. I struggled with theological lies that said tongues were from the devil. Simultaneously, I won a music scholarship, changed schools and developed a wonderful friendship with a Pentecostal. One day I said to my friend, 'I don't want to hear another thing about the Holy Spirit'. On reflection, she wasn't bombarding me, rather, I was under conviction! Today, though 1,000 miles apart, we remain prayer partners. What changed? I read *Prison to Praise* by Merlin Carothers. My resistance melted as I discovered the Holy Spirit, praise and miracles go together! Barrier #1 was down.

2. In the 1980s I married, had children and my calling in to music ministry began to flourish. Then one day, the bottom fell out of the ministry, and I felt my destiny shatter. I tell the story on Day 21 of this devotional, titled 'Bitter or Better'. In the midst of the confusion and pain, the Lord told me to praise Him. It changed my life and impacted me ever since. Barrier #2 came down as praise delivered me from disappointment and bitterness.

3. In the late 90s and crossing into the new millennium, I entered a new and important season of learning about and leading intercession and worship for our city. A small team often met behind locked doors. I felt my call and destiny were also locked up. Again, the Lord said to remain faithful in worship—many times this was with a heavy heart, travail, even frustration. Yet as I pursued Him in worship, angels and supernatural signs in the heavens appeared. Barrier #3 was removed by remaining faithful in praise. God 'suddenly' unlocked doors in Australia and overseas. I and some around me experienced supernatural joy. Soon after we pioneered our current ministry at *Tabernacle of David (Bendigo).*

4. In 2018 the Lord challenged our ministry team to embark on a 'Grumble Fast'. (See Day 7, 'Rescue From Enemies'.) Life was not crumbling, but there were many small irritations. But the Lord was seeking to position our hearts to receive His sudden supernatural intervention and help. I now realise Barrier #4 came down as a consequence of our 'Grumble Fast'. The Lord delivered our ministry from a destructive plot of Jezebel and Leviathan.

Having now done the 'Grumble Fast' three times, I will be honest—I still have to make a choice. But, I *have* become quicker to recognise and rectify pockets of grumbling. To sustain a 40-day fast we needed constant reminders. Hence, the concept of this book was born.

Developing a lifestyle of thanksgiving transformed my life. And it has enabled me to lead, teach and equip the Body of Christ in Throne-Room worship. As you commit to this 'Grumble Fast', I pray it will be as life- changing for you as it has been for me. Most of all, I pray you enjoy the delicious feast the Lord has prepared for you at His table—even if it's in the presence of His enemies. As you enter His courts with victorious praise, press right into His Glory realms.

Ruth Webb

Why 'Grumble Fast'?

When I mention the 'Grumble Fast' to people, most respond with a nervous laugh. It seems grumbling affects every human on the planet—even powerful spiritual leaders!

Grumbling is human nature. To complain and whinge is our default language! As Christians, we know we shouldn't. Yet we often excuse it because it's just being human. Or else we put on a mask and pretend we don't grumble. But oh dear, what if others could hear our internal self-talk?

Have you considered the serious consequences of grumbling? Or that it belongs to the old nature? A reminder of Israel in the wilderness reveals God's opinion of it and its deadly consequences.

Mark Virkler's research suggests that the thought life of most Christians is 90% negative! At first, I thought he was exaggerating. But as the Lord took me through this fast, I soon discovered the frequent gravitation towards grumbling. I then wondered if Mark Virkler's conclusion is conservative!

Science has proven grumbling impacts severely on relationships, sleep, physical pain and mental illness. They believe grumbling rewires our brain for negativity.[1] Yet that is not how God made us. He made us for love. And the atmosphere of heaven is praise.

So, how do we change?

Isaiah 58 Fast of the Lord

Fasting is a powerful way to deal with issues of the flesh. Yeshua said, '***when***' you fast, not '***if***' you fast. We often think of fasting as abstaining from food. Yet the fast of the Lord described in Isaiah 58 addresses the removal of yokes and bondages by means apart from food.

> *'Don't point your finger and **say** wicked things.' (Isaiah 58:9 GW)*

Why 40 Days?

Forty days are an important time period in Scripture and is associated with testing and trial. Rain fell for 40 days in the time of Noah's flood. The spies were in the Promised Land for 40 days before making their report. Israel spent 40 years in the wilderness. Nineveh was given 40 days to repent. King Saul and King David each reigned for 40 years. Jesus fasted 40 days in the wilderness to overcome Satan before being released into ministry.

As a music teacher, when bad habits have been 'practiced', it takes longer to undo the bad and to then establish correct habits. A memory pathway is ***established*** after seven repetitions. A habit takes 21 days to establish (3 lots of x 7 repetitions).

Bonus

If a habit takes 21 days, a lifestyle may take a little longer. Hopefully, by 40 days it's nearly a lifestyle!

We are giving you *two bonus days* to help establish your habit of praise. (42 days = 6 lots x 7 repetitions)

How It Works

Each day contains:

- A 5-10 minute reading with a specific Scriptural focus—including testimonies and brief teaching
- Activation
- Prayer

During these 40 days you will discover:

- The dangers of grumbling, and how it activates the devil
- 40 scriptural reasons to give thanks to God and discover the joy of feasting at His table of praise
- How to catch yourself complaining
- How to be grateful for everything
- How to create the atmosphere of heaven in your heart and home through habitual gratitude.

Praise is the power of heaven. Let this Teaching Devotional help you to navigate and overcome the significant daily battles of these end-days. Be strengthened and renewed as you focus on His promises, His character, His name, His Word, His power and His love.

Rejoice. God is good.

1.https://www.inc.com/jessica-stillman/complaining-rewires-your-brain-for-negativity-science-says.html

https://www.entrepreneur.com/article/281734

https://curiousmindmagazine.com/complaining-physically-rewires-your-brain/?fbclid=IwAR3g1vLrs8DrdBmWlnYk9M1zD9kV3eAGuF_ZovtPUZhVUYIYd7QjpedHfpg

How to Fast

Preparation

To get the most out of the 40-Day Grumble Fast, it is wise to prepare.

Do you want to find habits and strongholds of grumbling?

Do you want to enter a new and wonderful season of intimacy with the Lord?

Make a Commitment

You ***must commit*** to the 40 - Day fast. If you don't, the pressures of life will knock you out!

- Grab your calendar now! Mark 40 days that work for you. Or sign onto our Facebook page and find out how to receive a daily reminder on email.[2]
- Choose to ***fast*** from criticism, complaining and grumbling.
- Choose to ***give thanks*** until praise is a lifestyle.
- Consider joining with friends, family, or home group. Accountability to share victories and struggles is really helpful—especially when it gets tough.
- Commit to the best time of the day. Consider work schedules and sleep patterns. Allow time to read each day's material, (about 10 minutes) plus time to reflect, act and pray.[3]

- Buy or prepare a notebook. (Or, you can write notes in this book.) Each day record 3 things to be grateful for. Write down any tricky issues ***and*** record victories and revelations during the fast.

- Use Appendix 1-5 as you prepare to fast or at any time. They are helpful resources to use as a springboard to add your own Scriptures and tools. Appendix 5 is also helpful to guide non or new believers.

Prepare Your Heart

Israel spent three days cleansing themselves before meeting the Lord on Mount Sinai.[4] Before you fast, take a few days to prepare your heart. Work through the following questions before the Lord. If you are not sure, ask the Holy Spirit to help you.

Be Honest Before God

Consider these questions before the Lord. In your journal, be as specific as you can.

1. Are any circumstances troubling you? Identify any situations robbing your peace.

2. Write down any situations that keep you awake at night. Do any conversations or scenarios replay in your head like a broken record? Write them down.

3. Can you recognise and identify any negative self-talk?

4. Are there times you really want to worship the Lord, but a recurring situation distracts your attention?

Evaluate Your Concept of God versus Your Circumstances

Using your answers to questions 1-4, consider:

- Are any of these circumstances bigger than God?
- Can you still give the Lord thanks?
- Can you give thanks for these situations?

Note any reaction in your heart to each question.

How does your heart see God? (Be honest)

- If God is the Creator of the Universe, are your circumstances too hard for Him?
- Can you trust Him to work out these situations for your good?
- Is the blood of Jesus enough for your circumstances? Is His grace sufficient for you? Is His creative and resurrection power able to restore your life?
- If nothing can separate you from the love of Christ, how can these situations steal His love and shalom?
- If God is for you, who can be against you?
- At the cross, did Jesus destroy ***all*** the works the devil is using to try to destroy you?

If Jesus has made you more than a conqueror, then you are a champion with everything you need to defeat grumbling—and win!

Getting Ready for Day One!

The suggested way to work through each day:

1. Allow 5-10 minutes each day to read the Scripture, devotional, activation and prayer.

2. Work through the activation and prayer at your own pace. Take time to dialogue with Holy Spirit. Especially ask for keys to circumstances in which your peace has been (or is habitually) disturbed or robbed. Write them down.

3. Apply the promises to your day. Give thanks by declaring Scriptures over your circumstances. This will help to identify where grumbling is habitual and to break the habit.

4. Any time you struggle to give thanks, stop and ask Holy Spirit for keys. When the Holy Spirit convicts you of grumbling, repent according to 1 John 1:9. Then give thanks for His forgiveness and cleansing.

5. Break any agreements with lies of the enemy. Ask the Holy Spirit to help you to see the situation from His perspective.

6. Record and date encounters, revelation and answers to prayers of gratitude.

7. Review each day—how did it go? Give thanks for at least 3 things in that day. Increase the number as you can.

Now as you start, let me pray for you.

Righteous loving Father, bless Your precious people to experience a significant shift in their hearts and circumstances as they commit to fast grumbling. Holy Spirit, release a new spirit of praise on each one who does this fast—for Your glory and the exaltation of Your name. Draw each one closer into Your heart—to be extravagant lovers and worshippers of Holy God. Holy Spirit, anoint each one with Your *dunamis* power to overcome the world, the flesh and the devil. Open the eyes of each heart so they may encounter more of Your love.

[5]Father of glory, I pray You would impart the riches of the Spirit to each person, so they can know You through a deepening intimacy with You. I pray Your light will illuminate the eyes of their imagination, and flood them with light, until they experience the full revelation of the hope of Your calling. Amen

---

2. https://www.facebook.com/Grumble-Fast-108650737335781

3. Two Options:

   a.) Read the Scripture, devotional, activation and prayer in the morning. Consider it during the day. Before bed, review the day. Give thanks for 3 things. Make relevant notes in your journal

   OR

   b.) Start the day according to the Jewish calendar (each day begins at sunset). In the evening, read the day's Scripture, devotional, activation and prayer. Consider it throughout the night and next day, seeking the help of Holy Spirit. Give thanks for 3 things. Make relevant notes in your journal.

4. Exodus 19:1-11

5. Personalised adaption from Ephesians 1:17-19 TPT

DAY 1

Gratitude Is a Password

'Enter into His gates with thanksgiving, And into His courts with praise. Be thankful to Him, and bless His name.' (Psalm 100:4 NKJV)

The Passion Translation says we enter the Lord's gates 'with the password of praise.'

In this age of computers and cyberspace, we all need passwords. We need them to access emails, online banking, online shopping, and programs like Google, YouTube and the like. Everyone needs a password to get access. First you must sign up. Then you select a password, and each time you return, you enter the password and voila, you are in.

Our 'password' to the Presence of the Lord is praise and gratitude. Without it, we are denied access!

We 'sign up' when we are born again,[6] redeemed and cleansed by the blood of Jesus. Without that sign-up, our password is not recognised. Signing up is usually a one-time event. But we need a password every time we want access. And the only valid password into the Lord's Presence is gratitude.

The well known song of the 1970's began with the words, 'I will enter His gates with thanksgiving in my heart'.[7] The gates to His Presence open in response to ***hearts*** filled with gratitude. This Psalm in Hebrew suggests the involvement of singing. But before we sing a note, the posture of our hearts must be centred in thanks. Praise from the mouth without gratitude in the heart will make it difficult to open His gates—like an electronic gate when there is no power!

Language and Atmosphere of Heaven

Gratitude is the language of heaven. Language is the basis of accurate communications. The atmosphere or oxygen of heaven is songs of praise. On earth we die without oxygen. Our spirits wither and die without communing with our Lord in the rarefied atmosphere of praise.

If gratitude and grumbling are like a language, what language are you speaking? If gratitude is the language of heaven, where does the language of grumbling come from?

If praise creates the atmosphere of heaven, what atmosphere does grumbling build? What atmosphere is being created in your home?

Whatever your current circumstances, can you give thanks to the Lord? He is your Creator, Saviour, Redeemer, Holy One of Israel and soon coming King! He is good. His love never fails.

Grumbling Is Easy. Praise Is a Sacrifice!

Despite your circumstances, what can you thank Him for today?

When we give thanks for small things, it helps us to see and appreciate—He is Immanuel, 'God is with us'. Gratitude and thanksgiving invite God into our day. A spark of hope is lit. Faith rises.

When our children were young, the evening bedtime ritual was a story and prayer, which began with them finding three things to be thankful for. They would thank the Lord for food, a warm bed and a wonderful array of things we adults often miss. No wonder praise is perfected in the mouth of children. These became precious and memorable times together.

Science has proven the Bible is right. Giving thanks for the smallest things shifts attitudes. Daily gratitude improves mental health.

Choose to log into your heavenly account. If you want to enter His Presence, the only way in is through His gates of gratitude and praise!

ACTIVATION

- Start your journal today.
- Record ***at least*** 3-5 things you are grateful for.
- Do this for the 40 days, and you will soon discover new realms of His Presence. Joy will fill your day; and watch for the changes in your attitude.

What can you give thanks for today?

If you have a bed to sleep in and a roof over your head—give thanks.

If you have food in your stomach—give thanks.

If you have safe and clean water to drink—give thanks.

If you have peace in your heart—give thanks.

If you have people in your life who love you and care for you—give thanks.

There are millions who would love to have some of the above.

PRAYER

Father God, I honour Your Holy name. I thank You that by the precious blood of Yeshua, I am redeemed and I am Your child. I am so grateful that Your blood on the Mercy Seat allows me into Your Presence. You are worthy of praise. I am amazed; You are the powerful King of the Universe, yet You love and care for me. You are gentle and kind yet also righteous and holy. Amen

Continue speaking to Him from your heart as you contemplate His amazing grace.

---

6. "He Has Made Me Glad" by Leona Von Brethorst
Lyrics © 1974 Universal Music Publishing Group

7. The terms 'born again' and 'redeemed' are defined and explained in Appendix 5. They may sound like jargon to non-Christians, but they are Biblical terms. Appendix 5 is for those who are unsure of the meanings, and for those who may be reading this book but have not, or are unsure if they have 'signed up' yet.

8. Psalm 78:40-43, Psalm 95:7-9 and Psalm 106:14-25

DAY 2

Grumbling Limits God

'All the tests they (Israel) endured on their way through the wilderness are... an example that provides us with a warning so that we can learn through what they experienced. For we live in a time when the purpose of all the ages past is now completing its goal within us. So beware if you think it could never happen to you, lest your pride becomes your downfall.' (1 Corinthians 10:11,12 TPT)

An aerial view is vastly different than one at ground level. If we were to view our circumstances from God's perspective, I wonder what they would look like? What does our praise or our grumbling sound like to God?

Paul gave a solemn warning to the Corinthian Church and to us. The warning is based on Israel's journey through the wilderness. Despite being miraculously delivered from Egypt, what did Israel do? Grumble.

Even though Hollywood considered Israel's deliverance from Egypt worthy of the big screen—Israel was ungrateful, and their ingratitude turned a 10-day journey into 40 years! Exposed to the destroyer, Israel no longer had God's hand of protection over them.[8] I wonder how history will speak of our journey?

The differences between gratitude and grumbling are stark. They expose the war between our flesh and the Holy Spirit:

Gratitude honours God. Grumbling dishonours God.

Praise disarms the devil. Grumbling empowers the devil.

Praise activates God's favour. Grumbling hinders God's help!

Grumbling is devastating to God and man. Even science has concluded that grumbling has negative impacts upon relationships, sleep and health. 'When you complain, your body releases the stress hormone cortisol'.[9] But gratitude aids healing and relationships.

Three sombre truths for us to learn from Israel's grumbling:

1. Grumbling Grieves and Wounds God

> *'How they grieved Him with their grumblings... Continually they turned back from Him and provoked the Holy One of Israel!' (Psalm 78:40b,41 TPT)*

Commentary from *The Passion Translation* suggests Israel's behaviour actually 'wounded the heart of God'. Ouch! How sad and grievous is that? Genuine lovers of God do not want to wound the Holy One of Israel!

Ingratitude brings sorrow to the heart of every parent who has sacrificially poured love into their children. Nothing hurts a giving parent more than a whinging child. How does our grumbling impact our heavenly Father?

Yet, doesn't a grateful child make our heart sing? No wonder the Lord wants us to bring Him our *true and sincere thanks.* Jesus spoke of the one grateful leper who returned with gratitude.

2. Grumbling Limits God

> *'Again and again they limited God, preventing Him from blessing them.' (Psalm 78:41 TPT)*

It may seem strange, but there are several things God cannot do!

- He cannot lie.
- He cannot sin.
- He cannot break His Word or His covenants.
- And He cannot bless us when we grumble!

Grumbling is like shooting ourselves in the foot. It limits and impedes God. Grumbling is a roadblock to His blessing!

Praise is the atmosphere of heaven—not grumbling! Gratitude is a governing law of the universe. Gratitude invites Him into our situation and opens the way to blessing.

3. Grumbling Leads to Rebellion and Unbelief.

Grumbling not only opens doors to demonic interference, but also leads us to rebellion and unbelief. It is a slippery slope that Israel slid down.

> *'Our fathers in Egypt did not understand Your wonders;*
> *They did not remember the multitude of Your mercies,*
> *But rebelled by…the Red Sea.' (Psalm 106:7)*

Do you struggle with grumbling, rebellion or unbelief? Do a health check on your self-talk; are you grateful or complaining?

If the Lord inhabits the praises of His people, who inhabits grumbling?

> *'Bring Yahweh praise and you will find Him. Your hearts will overflow with life forever!' (Psalm 22:26 TPT)*

ACTIVATION

Today, you have a choice—to honour or dishonour. Remember, gratitude from the heart:

- Honours the Lord and gives Him joy—especially in our day of testing.
- Invites Him into our trial.
- Terminates consent with the devil and aligns us with God.
- Boosts faith and hope—especially when life is tough!
- Aids our obedience to God's Word and aligns us with His character and His throne.
- Is fundamental to the worship of Yahweh.

PRAYER

Lord God Almighty, You are Elohim, Adonai, El Shaddai. I am so grateful Your mercies are new every morning. Today I come to Your mercy seat.

I repent of grieving Your heart through my grumbling. *(Be specific and honest in your prayers.)*

I repent for limiting You from helping me in these circumstances. *(Again, be specific and honest.)*

I repent for believing and agreeing with the lies of the devil. I renounce and break all agreement with the devil. I choose to believe and receive Your truth.

I repent of my rebellion against You, and my duplicity of believing but not believing. *(Again, be specific and honest in your prayers.)* Amen

- Take communion and allow His blood to cleanse Your soul from these sins.
- When we confess our sin, He is faithful to forgive *and* to cleanse us. Thank Him.

Give thanks—today is a new day!

---

9. 'How Complaining Rewires Your Brain for Negativity' https://www.entrepreneur.com/article/281734

DAY 3

Prelude to Worship

'Come before His presence with singing...Enter into His gates with thanksgiving, And into His courts with praise.'(Psalm 100:2, 4 NKJV)

Psalm 100 is titled 'A Psalm of Thanksgiving'. It's a call to enter the Lord's Presence according to His protocols. If gratitude and praise are a *password* to get access *into* His presence, consider songs of praise like a 'prelude' as we come through His outer courts.

In music, a 'Prelude' is usually a short piece to preface a larger work like a symphony or opera.[10] Hearts filled with gratitude will *overflow* into songs of thanks and praise. A heart filled with gratitude cannot be silent. And true songs of praise do not come from grumbling hearts! Gratitude and praise begin the journey. They give us access through the gates and into the outer court. Songs of praise are also the starting point, the prelude, the introduction to which He will then take us deeper into His Presence, His Throne-Room and higher levels of intimacy, worship and the glory. The Father desires and seeks out true worshippers. The first step is a heart attitude of gratitude to both big ***and*** small issues of life.

Shifting Gratitude from Head to Heart Is not Easy!

In the *Preface* I briefly outlined my life journey to become a worship leader. Every milestone of my life has involved a challenging encounter with the Lord to choose thanksgiving over grumbling. Each milestone was not just a test, but rather became my personal *Prelude to Worship*.

In the late 1980s—early 1990s, as I daily chose thanksgiving over anger, heartache and depression, the concept of thanksgiving gradually shifted from a mental assent to a heart reality. Assenting to truth in our head is much easier than knowing it by experience. Giving thanks was easy when life had few or small hurdles. But when facing major disappointment and heartache, it is much harder.

While the distance between our physical head and heart is about 12-15 inches, the emotional distance is *much* further! Shifting thanksgiving from my head to heart was not fast or easy. It took months and months of daily obedience. But those hours of praising in the midst of heartache have become the most treasured and precious memories as I drew nearer to Him. I appreciated Him in deeper ways, learned from Him, and was healed in His Presence. He taught me the correlation of heart gratitude and worship in spirit and truth! He taught me ***how*** to lead worship, and how to adapt my musical skills to move in His holy river. Eventually, we were able to make a huge transition into our current ministry.

Gratitude Is Not a Random Command.

Our Creator fashioned the world to function on love and gratitude. Earth was meant to be the worship centre of the universe. We are wired for love. Gratitude and praise are part of the love language.

As Christians we face an emotional challenge. We 'know' we should give thanks. It's scriptural. But *how* do we do this from our hearts when our hearts are breaking? How to praise when life is tough, unfair and really hurts?

Thanksgiving is not about our circumstances, or about us. Thanksgiving is all about Him and who He is. Thanksgiving places the focus on His perfect character, which is not impacted by our stuff.

Saturate Your Day in Prayer

What keeps you distracted from praise? What is it that pulls you in a different direction? What keeps you bogged down in the old nature? Prayer is the solution to the tug of war.

> *'Be saturated in prayer throughout each day, offering your faith-filled requests before God with overflowing gratitude. Tell him every detail of your life.' (Philippians 4: 6 TPT)*

In your prayer and praise today, be truthful and honest with the Lord. Don't try to hide stuff—He already knows! As you offer up your circumstances to Him today, thank Him for His Presence, His goodness, and His answers.

Choice to Come up Higher

Giving praise is a choice we make ***every*** day. Essentially, it's a choice between our old and new nature. Grumbling belongs to the sin nature. Praise belongs to our new nature.

> *'For the law of the Spirit of life in Christ Jesus has made me free from the law of sin and death'. (Romans 8:2 NKJV)*

The law of lift supersedes the law of gravity and allows birds and aeroplanes to fly. So too the law of the Spirit supersedes the law of sin and death and enables us to walk, live and worship in the Holy Spirit—thus winning the battle between these two natures!

On days of severe loss or disappointment, the tug-of-war between the two natures may seem more turbulent. When life goes pear-shaped, we still have to choose. We can run to His loving Presence as our safe place[11], we can grit our teeth to survive, or we can get angry that God did not protect us from 'x, y or z'. And some days we may oscillate between all three!

Gratitude rhymes with 'attitude,' and it comes from the Latin word *gratus,* which means 'thankful' or 'pleasing. [12]The catchphrase 'gratitude—attitude—altitude' deliberately progresses in that order. Feasting on gratitude shifts our attitude. And a changed attitude lifts our altitude. Gratitude defies emotional gravity so we can lift off, soar in the Spirit and come up to His altitude!

I pray this 'Grumble Fast' becomes a catalyst for you to deal with any pockets of habitual grumbling and unlock the door into higher and deeper dimensions of worship in His Presence. As John heard the call, 'Come up here'. (Revelation 4:1)

ACTIVATION

1. Saturate your circumstances in prayer. As you make your requests to God; tell him every detail.
2. Find 3-5 things to be thankful for today.
3. Give thanks. Find songs of praise you can sing today. Tell Him how grateful you are for who He is and for His Presence in the midst of life.

PRAYER

Holy Spirit, I am so grateful You help me to become a true worshipper. Thank You for Your help today. I praise You. You help me overcome my propensity to grumble. Thank You, Holy Spirit, for Your breath lifting me up on Your wings and lifting me up into the spiritual thermals and currents today. Amen

Pray in the Spirit for as long as you can.

Ask: *Lord, show me; 'what does my heart look like from Your perspective'? Have I been complaining and grumbling rather than praising You?*

Be still. Wait and listen in His Presence.

Spend time in repentance to re-align your heart attitude and altitude.

Now spend time praising Him and being lifted up and above your circumstances.

10. Sometimes, however, especially in the Romantic period of music, 'Preludes' are stand alone pieces.

11. Psalm 16:1

12. https://www.vocabulary.com/dictionary/gratitude

DAY 4

Sacrifice of Praise

'I will offer to You the sacrifice of thanksgiving...I will pay my vows to the Lord...In the courts of the Lord's house.' (Psalm 116:17-19 NKJV)

'Surrender yourselves to God to be his sacred, living sacrifices. And live in holiness...for this becomes your genuine expression of worship.' (Romans 12:1 TPT)

'Let us continually offer the sacrifice of praise to God, that is, the fruit of our lips, giving thanks to His name.' (Hebrews 13:15 NKJV)

Today's Scriptures are based on the concept of the 'sacrifice of praise'. We often think this means giving thanks in the midst of tough circumstances. While it is good and true to do this, there is much more to the phrase 'sacrifice of praise'.

Biblically, the 'sacrifice of thanksgiving' was part of the sacrificial system in the Tabernacle and Temple. There were five offerings within the sacrificial system:

1. Burnt offering
2. Meal or grain offering
3. Peace, fellowship or thank offering: (often connected with vows)[13]
4. Sin offering
5. Guilt or trespass offering.

Each offering was a shadow of the sacrifice of Jesus on the cross, and each one is about intimate relationship between God and mankind.

Peace or Thank Offering

The thank offering is first found in Leviticus 3 and 7:11-36. The terms for the offering are often interchanged, depending upon the Bible Dictionary or commentary you use; peace offering, thank offering, sacrifice of thanksgiving and vow offering![14]

A thank offering was to bring a sweet savour to the Lord. A sweet savour means to enjoy food or an experience. To savour something means you take it slowly to bask in its joy and enjoy every mouthful or moment. What a picture of the sweetness we experience today as we offer praise and worship and truly commune in His Presence.

The thank offering was usually offered when the worshipper had experienced a miracle of healing or some major breakthrough. For example, when Hannah gave birth to Samuel.

When King David brought the Ark into Jerusalem, he offered burnt offerings *and* peace-thank offerings. These represented total surrender, shedding of blood for forgiveness and access to the Lord; a covenant of peace and expressions of gratitude for victory over the Jebusites and the Lord's Presence being successfully brought into the heart of Jerusalem. Shifting the Ark into Jerusalem was a story worthy of great jubilation and rejoicing.

A covenant of peace was made by sacrificing cattle, a lamb or goat. If it was specifically for a thanksgiving offering, then unleavened cakes and bread were also offered. These were eaten by both God and man. God consumed His portion by fire. The priest and the one offering the sacrifice ate their portions in the Presence of the Lord. It signified deep and sweet fellowship between God and the giver.

On Day 2 we noted that science correlates gratitude with health and good relationships. These are all concepts within the true meaning of peace, or *shalom* in Hebrew. It is no surprise the thank or peace offerings are connected. Gratitude positions our heart for His shalom. (See Day 19 'Shalom' for further insight.)

Fruit of Our Lips

The *sacrifice of praise* becomes even more amazing when we discover the writer to the Hebrews says this sacrifice is fulfilled by what comes from our mouths. *The Passion Translation* powerfully brings our attention to the link between the original sacrifice of animals and cakes and the fulfilment of it being praise from our mouths.

> *'So we no longer offer up a steady stream of blood sacrifices, but through Jesus, we will offer up to God a steady stream of praise sacrifices—these are "the lambs" we offer from our lips that celebrate his name!' (Hebrews 13:15 TPT)*

The sacrifice of praise from our lips is something that God enjoys so much; it is sweet to His ears and heart. He loves to bask in it. Sacrifice of praise indicates we are having sweet communion with the Lord—feasting together at His table. The emphasis of the sacrifice of praise is not about how hard it is for us to do, but rather, the joy of communion both for God and the one who offers the sacrifice.

Psalm 110 speaks of Messiah subduing all His enemies by shattering their strongholds. In the midst of these battles, it seems He gains His strength from the love and worship of His people!

> *'Your people will be Your love offerings, In the day of Your mighty power You will be exalted...Yet He himself will drink from his inheritance as from a flowing brook; refreshed by love He will stand victorious!' (Psalm 110:3,7 TPT)*

Thanksgiving Is an Offering

Our modern church culture thinks of offerings as being a monetary gift. While buying the finest animals to sacrifice and the finest flour and oil to make bread and cakes would require finances, the sacrifice of thanksgiving is not primarily about finance. Thanksgiving from the heart is the offering. As indicated in Hebrews, the offering is the praise from our lips. This is not just 'lip service' devoid of a grateful heart, because Jesus called that scenario vain worship! (Matthew 15) A true thank offering is a grateful heart overflowing out of our lips.

Again, our modern church culture often thinks songs of praise are for our pleasure. But for the **giver** of the biblical thank offering, thanksgiving is primarily for His benefit, not ours. Yes, we benefit from the sweet fellowship we enjoy with Him. But it begins with us giving Him an offering of praise. We cannot really offer true thanksgiving if we are only doing it for our own benefit.

It can be very costly to offer the sacrifice of praise, but the motivation is totally love, and it is always voluntary. Like Mary breaking the alabaster box, we willingly pour thanks ***onto*** the Lord.[15] Regardless of personal circumstances, we surrender ourselves and offer thanks as a gift, as an act of worship. Some days it may be more costly.

Thanksgiving - todah

The Hebrew word for thanksgiving is *todah*[16], meaning praise, give thanks, extend the hand in adoration, a choir of worshippers.

A corporate expression of praise, or 'choir of worshippers' becomes extremely powerful when each person in the 'choir' has first learned to offer their own personal and private thank offering to the Lord. The choir of worshippers the Lord is seeking are *whole congregations*, not just worship teams. **A worship team cannot worship for you!** The Lord is looking for worshippers whose grateful hearts overflow through lips filled with praise and hands extended in adoration. For these are the worshippers who release the sounds of heaven and frequencies of the glory!

ACTIVATION

As you consider this revelation about the sacrifice of praise, ask the Holy Spirit to lead you today.

- What is the best offering of praise you can give Him today?
- Set aside time to give that offering, and for it to be a sweet savour. Allow time for your offering to be enjoyed by Him. Allow time in His Presence to enjoy sweet communion with Him.

PRAYER

'Lord, because I am your loving servant, You have broken open my life and freed me from my chains. Now I'll worship you passionately and bring to you my sacrifice of praise, drenched with thanksgiving!' (Psalm 116:16,17 TPT) Amen

---

13. Exact titles vary according to translation. Some translations call them fellowship offerings.
14. Leviticus 7:12-15 Psalm 107:22 Amos 4:5
15. Leviticus 22:29 The sacrifice of thanksgiving was to be offered 'at your own will'.
16. Strong's Concordance – Hebrew 8426 *todah*

DAY 5

Grumbling, Spirit of Forgetting and Jezebel

'You freed them [Israel] from the strong power of those who oppressed them and rescued them from bondage... Seeing this, the people believed Your words, and they all broke out with songs of praise! Yet how quickly they forgot Your miracles of power.' (Psalm 106:10–13 TPT)

Immediately after getting to the other side of the Red Sea, Israel had a whopping praise gathering. They celebrated their miraculous deliverance. But shortly afterward, tragedy hit. They forgot the miracle at the Red Sea! How can you forget such a momentous miracle? Tragically, Israel did. Consequently, they started grumbling.

They not only forgot the miracles, they also forgot the God of miracles!

'They forgot God their Savior, Who had done great things in Egypt' (Psalm 106:21 NKJV)[17]

How Israel forgot their Saviour is hard to understand. Yet I have had people tell me of amazing encounters they have had with the Lord—and then promptly forgot them! How could this be?

Spirit of Forgetting

In her book, *Dealing with Ziz: the Spirit of Forgetting,* Anne Hamilton suggests there is a spirit called Ziz, whose assignment is to help us forget God. Anne suggests the spirit of forgetting seeks to shred and dismember truth, causing us to forget God, and is the power source behind Jezebel and every lure to Baal worship.[18] This makes sense when you read Scriptures like Judges 3:7 and Jeremiah 18:15: '*So the children of Israel …forgot the Lord their God, and served the Baals and Asherahs*'. '*Because My people have forgotten Me, They have burned incense to worthless idols.*'

If idolatry is a consequence of forgetting God, then clearly a demon is involved in the process. A malevolent supernatural force is the only reasonable explanation for God's people forgetting His goodness and miraculous power. It is the only explanation for God's people believing lies and being seduced to worship hideous false gods. Forgetting God is not simply due to brain fog, age, or busyness.

So how do we overcome the spirit of forgetting? How do we defeat Ziz and Jezebel? How do we remember God's goodness? One major key is giving thanks! Yes, there are other factors as many good books on the subject will tell you. But never underestimate praise being the power of heaven to deliver us even from the spirit of forgetting!

As we give thanks, we are reminded of God's goodness and miracles—thus we ***remember*** Him. Giving thanks aids and accelerates healing as we invite God into our situation. Gratitude activates memories and angels! Gratitude helps us align with truth and thus remove legal ground from the enemy, removing Jezebel's lure to forget Yahweh.

Remembrance and Praise

When Israel reached the other side of the Red Sea, they immediately burst into song. Miriam and the women danced with tambourines and sang the song of Moses. Faith fuelled their victorious celebration filled with rejoicing, praise, and exaltation. (Exodus 15:1-20) They even sang prophetic proclamations about their destiny into the Promised Land.

> *'You will bring them in and plant them In the mountain of Your inheritance...' (Exodus 15:17 NKJV)*

Yet within three days they were grumbling! Marah, the place of bitter waters, tested them. Sadly, they 'forgot' the miracles and grumbled.

How easy it is to be thankful when we experience breakthroughs, yet as soon as the testings come, we fall into grumbling? One time I was reading 1 Corinthians 10, and in my heart, I was critical of Israel's forgetful behaviour in the wilderness. '*What losers*,' I said to myself. Suddenly, the Holy Spirit challenged me; 'You are no different than them'! And this was the precise point of Paul's address—we need to learn from their mistakes. How easily we grumble in the wilderness of life.

The consequence of grumbling was costly for Israel and is costly for us. Grumbling causes us to:

- Forget God's miracles
- Forget God's promises
- Forget God's love

- Believe and agree with the devil's lies
- Align with the devil's plans
- Forget God Himself and even stray to worship other gods
- Be subjected to destruction by demonic powers

Consider Paul's sober warning about grumbling.

> *'And don't grumble, as some of them did, and were destroyed by the Destroying Angel.' (1 Corinthians 10:10 CJB)*[19]

Gods' Perspective of Egypt and Pharaoh

What if Israel could have seen their slavery from God's viewpoint? Yahweh had appointed Israel to remain in Egypt for ***exactly*** 430 years (Exodus 12:40-41). What if they could have remembered God's promise to Abraham[20] (Genesis 15:13-14), counted the years and given thanks that their slavery was nearly over? They would have then recognised Moses as their deliverer.

God has no 'accidents'. El Shaddai gave Abraham and Moses promises that Israel could hang onto. Even Pharaoh had a purpose:

> *'I put you here for this reason: to demonstrate My power through you and to spread My name throughout the earth.' (Romans 9:17 GW)*

What if we could remember and give thanks for the prophetic words to help us through our trials? What if we could believe God for a higher purpose for our painful events? Can we trust Him that our suffering is not in vain?

The focus of our eyes determines the response of our heart. Israel's eyes were fixed on their pain and their harsh tyrannical ruler.

However valid, grumbling exacerbates pain—it is the language and handcuffs of the devil. When Israel forgot Yahweh, they allowed hopelessness to try to sabotage their deliverance and destiny.

Gratitude lifts our eyes to the glory and the lifter of our head. Gratitude lifts our eyes above our circumstances so we can see our Creator, Redeemer and the Author and Finisher of our faith. Remember His Word, His acts and who He is—faithful, kind, true, and merciful. When we turn our eyes upon Jesus 'the things of earth will grow strangely dim in the light of His glory and grace!'[21]

ACTIVATION

1. Continue to keep a diary as you work through these forty days of gratitude. Record and document your testimony: revelations from Holy Spirit, things you need to deal with, and miracles that occur along the journey. Remember what He has done for you through the *Grumble Fast* and as you *Feast on Gratitude.*

2. Make the choice of Colossians 3:1-3 (TPT) and then pray this personalised version.

   'Lord, today I choose to set my mind on things above rather than on the things currently happening in my life. I thank You Jesus; because You died, my life is hidden in You. Messiah, when You return, I will also appear with You in glory.'

PRAYER

Spend time praying in your heavenly language.

Recall and write down three miracles God has done for you. As you remember—give thanks!

Ask Holy Spirit to show you any grumbling you need to repent of.

Ask Holy Spirit to help you remember previous powerful encounters with His love, His grace, and protection. Thank Him for those experiences with His love and grace.

Rejoice in Him.

Proclaim His nature and goodness—He is your Creator, Saviour, Healer, Deliverer, Prince of Peace.

---

17. Also Psalm 78:11, Psalm 106:11-13
18. Anne Hamilton: *Dealing with Ziz: Spirit of Forgetting*, Armour Books
19. I recommend a good read of Psalm 78, Psalm 106, 1 Corinthians 10
20. Genesis 15: 13-14; Acts 7:6-7; Galatians 3:17
21. "Turn Your Eyes Upon Jesus" Written by Helen H. Lemmel, 1922 © Public Domain

DAY 6

Gratitude, Memory—Reason for Psalmists

'And he [King David] appointed some of the Levites to minister before the ark of the Lord, to commemorate, to thank, and to praise the Lord God of Israel.' (1 Chronicles 16:4 NKJV)

'...do not forget my teachings, and keep my commands in mind, because they will bring you long life, good years, and peace.' (Proverbs 3:1,2 GW)

After King David successfully brought the Ark into Jerusalem, he appointed prophet psalmists to lead praise 24/7. Their fulltime job description was to 'record, give thanks and praise'. The Hebrew word for 'record' is *zakar* and it means to mark, to mention, and to ***remember.*** Their songs of praise were to give thanks, but also by recording what God had done, they would help Israel to remember God—His goodness, His Word and His miracles.

Just as the role of musicians in David's Tabernacle was to help Israel praise God for His miracles, so too, worship leaders and worship teams today are facilitators for the Body of Messiah to remember and praise the Lord for His goodness. *Do **not*** minimise this important role. In a day of increasing stresses, it is powerful to join with other believers to be reminded of God's power and promises, and turn eyes and hearts to Him and away from the problems. The power of corporate singing to remember the goodness of God should not be underestimated.

In David's Tabernacle, thanksgiving was offered 24/7. The devil accuses believers 24/7. Praising the Lord 24/7 is powerful and necessary counter action. Nor should remembering be done just once—it must be repeated. Repetition is vital to establish neural pathways. Hence, as a teacher and musician, skills have to be practiced repeatedly. Repeated heartfelt thanksgiving is hygienic for body and soul. Our Creator knows that our brains and bodies function better when gratitude is a lifestyle.

The Seven Feasts of the Lord

The seven Feasts of the Lord are called *memorials* (Exodus 12:14) or *convocations* (Leviticus 23:2).

As a *memorial* they are related to the role of David's musicians. The root of the Hebrew word for *memorial* is *zakar*, the same word mentioned above, for the psalmists to 'record and give thanks' (1 Chronicles 16:4). Both the Feasts and David's musicians were to help Israel remember and give thanks for what the Lord had done.

As a *convocation*, the Feasts are a public gathering and a 'rehearsal'. As a musician, a rehearsal is going over what you are about to perform; you 'repeat or recite what has already been said or written.'[22] The Lord's Feasts recite the past miracles of God, while anticipating what He will repeat or do again.[23]

In Israel today, the Feasts are 'high holidays' where families and synagogues gather together to remember God, His past and future acts. Every year is a cycle of seven Feasts. The Feasts of the Lord help Jews and Gentiles to understand and remember the complete work of salvation. For example; Passover remembers the miracle of Israel being delivered from Egypt and also reminds believers that the feast was fulfilled by Jesus the Passover Lamb who delivered us out of the hand of the devil. And during His final Passover meal, Yeshua instituted what we Gentile believers call communion and told us to '***remember***' His death and resurrection.

So, there is a strong connection between the Feasts and Davidic musicians. Prophetically, this connection is an important fact for the Church to grasp. Combining these two factors, celebrating the Feasts and appointing Davidic musicians will release the Body of Christ into a higher level of victory and maturity.

'Remember' – 'Don't forget'!

The word 'remember' is used around 150 times in Scripture. It is reassuring to read the Lord say; 'He remembers His covenants'! He does not forget!

But us remembering Him is harder—it is a spiritual battle! The enemy wants us to forget God and sends a 'spirit of forgetting' to assist us. The Lord has given us the Holy Spirit to help, and He exhorts us to remember every instance He has intervened in our life.

To Israel He said;

'***Remember*** when you came out of Egypt (Exodus 13:3), ***remember*** what the Lord did to Pharaoh (Deuteronomy 7:18), ***remember*** the way the Lord brought you through the wilderness

(Deuteronomy 8:2), ***remember*** the Sabbath day is holy (Exodus 20:8), ***remember*** the name of the Lord (Psalm 30:7), ***remember*** the works of the Lord (Psalm 77:11), ***remember*** His love (Song of Solomon 1:4).'

Jesus and Paul spoke of remembering. These three are critical for us in this battle for memory;

1. In the institution of communion Jesus said, 'Do this in remembrance of Me' (Luke 22:19 NKJV). Take communion daily.

2. Jesus said the Holy Spirit would help us remember all the things He taught (John 14:26). When we struggle to remember His words, ask for the help of Holy Spirit. Ask for keys to your forgetting. Have you spoken death over your memory with word curses like 'I have a bad memory'? Do your memories need healing?

3. Paul encouraged Timothy (and us) to remember the resurrection of Jesus (2 Timothy 2:8). Apply resurrection life to memory.

We too should remember specific instances the goodness of God has touched us. Here are five ways to commit to deliberate action.

1. Celebrate the Feasts of the Lord throughout the year.
2. Participate frequently in corporate praise gatherings, at least weekly. God gave Israel a weekly day for worship (Sabbath), to rest and remember their Creator and deliverer. (Deuteronomy 5:15 GW)
3. Celebrate communion daily.
4. Teach God's Word to future generations. 'He commanded our forefathers to ***teach... their children***...God's ways will be ***passed down from one generation to the next...In this way***, every generation... will ***never forget*** the faithful ways

of God.' (Psalm 78:6-8 TPT) When our children were in a Christian school, the Lord challenged us that this was still mainly our responsibility as parents and not to leave it to the school.

5. Doing this 'Grumble Fast' is a deliberate action. As you record the daily encounters with the Lord and develop habitual gratitude, faith will arise in your heart.

The Passion Translation renders Proverbs 3:1, '***Never forget*** the things that I've taught you'. ***Never forget*** is for good reasons. This book provides reminders of some of those reasons. Remember His Word, His promises, His ways, His truth, His history, His miraculous blessings—these are the basis of thanksgiving! Remembering Him will help you to overcome the enemy, the 'spirit of forgetting'; provide you with 'long life, good years, and peace'; and maybe, even help with natural memories!

ACTIVATION

1) As you keep a diary for this forty-day fast, it will help you to 'remember' what God has done for you. Write down how He has blessed you today and give thanks!
2) Thank the Lord for the gift of memory. Rejoice that He has created every cell and organ with memory.
3) Place your hands on your head (or body) and bless your memory: 'I bless my memory' that it would function as God intended. Ask the Lord to heal and erase trauma and grief from stored memories. Bless your body to remember His goodness, kindness and miracles.

PRAYER

Creator of heaven and earth, Righteous Father, I bless You today. Thank You for the simple keys to victory in remembering You and giving thanks!

I repent of the times I have forgotten You—and focused on failures and distresses. I repent of forgetting Your miraculous works, Your truth and Your promises.

Holy Spirit, You are the helper. I ask for Your assistance in establishing gratitude as a habit. Show me any strongholds the enemy has gained in my memory.

I am so grateful that You never forget Your covenants and Your promises. You never leave, forsake or forget me. Hallelujah! Amen

Rejoice in His Presence.

---

22. https://www.etymonline.com/search?q=rehearse

23. Please note: according to Leviticus 23:2 the feasts are called "The feasts of the LORD". Some people mistakenly call them the feasts of Israel.
This mistake has created difficulties for some Gentile believers to recognise the significance of the feasts. The Feasts of the Lord are vital for Christians because they are fulfilled in the work of Jesus on the cross and when He returns.

DAY 7

Rescue from Enemies—Even Jezebel or Isis!

'He rescues me from my enemies... This is why I thank God with high praises!' (Psalm 18:48, 49 TPT)

'You shall surround me with songs of deliverance.' (Psalm 32:7 NKJV)

'Magnify the Lord... let us exalt His name ***together****... He heard me, And delivered me from all my fears... Many are the afflictions of the righteous, But the Lord delivers him out of them* ***all****.' (Psalms 34:3-6, 19 NKJV)*

What enemies do you face today? Fear, intimidation, shame, guilt, sickness, injury, poverty, failure, addictions, confusion, anxiety, division, accusation, betrayal, anger, isolation, hopelessness, loss, or death?

The Lord Is Our Deliverer.

Songs of praise, in the face of the enemy, activate deliverance. Songs of praise offend the devil. Songs of praise defeat the devil.

Songs of praise unite heaven and earth in victory.[24] As the enemy displays more hatred and anger in this season, raising the intensity of praise is key to victory.

Dream About ISIS

In 2014, ISIS suddenly became a threat. Within days, the Lord gave me a vivid dream.

A congregation of about 500 people had been in worship. Suddenly an ISIS gang burst into the meeting. Dressed in trademark black and their weapons cocked, around six ISIS warriors stood at the front of the church yelling vile curses and threats. The congregation fell silent as shock and terror gripped the worshippers.

After a while, a solitary lady in the middle of the congregation began to quietly declare: 'Salvation belongs to our God who sits on the throne, Jesus is Messiah, He is King of kings and Lord of lords, He reigns forever...'

Those in the immediate vicinity were at first surprised. But some gained courage from her action and began to quietly join her. There was no 'script'. But amazingly, everyone spontaneously spoke the same thing in unison. Gradually more and more of the congregation joined in as people grew in boldness and courage. The decrees became stronger and louder. Eventually, *everyone* in the congregation were declaring and singing loudly with conviction and courage, the goodness, power and majesty of King Yeshua. At that very moment—the ISIS group vaporised! They were gone!'

The Lord is showing us that the status quo church can be infiltrated and intimidated by the enemy. Church as usual, even praise, is not sufficient for the challenges we face today. God's people will not be able to rely solely on a small band of passionate, exuberant, even 'crazy' worshippers. Victory over intimidation in this season requires *every* believer to come up higher in praise. Songs of deliverance are not limited to the worship team. God's army has no passengers. The watchmen will sing, and must sing, **together**.[25]

'Grumble Fast' & Deliverance from Jezebelic Assignment

I thought I had learned the lessons about thanksgiving. But in 2018, the Lord challenged our whole ministry to a 40-day *Grumble Fast*.

Prior to this, a prophet friend had given me a word about the Lord sovereignly intervening in ways we had not witnessed before. I wasn't aware of our need for 'intervention', nor that I was grumbling. But as we embarked on our 40-day fast, I soon discovered how often I 'grumbled'—either out loud or especially silently! Becoming aware of the amount of negative self-talk was rather confronting!

I may have learned to give thanks when life was crumbling badly, but what about when life was just full of irritations? You know, those daily issues that annoy, distract and exasperate us? They may not be big, but they can accumulate, distract us and entice us to grumble.

After doing one 40-day fast, the Lord immediately told us to do another 40-days! I began to discern the enemy subtly drawing us away from our vision and call and sowing seeds of division and discord. We desperately needed the *Grumble Fast* to posture our hearts to receive God's miracles.

Suddenly, things shifted. Our whole group began to overcome

personal and corporate challenges. It was only in hindsight that we understood the enormity of the Lord's rescue. In fact, it was only in preparing this book for publication, that the Lord revealed we had been fighting a plan of Jezebel to destroy.

As we corporately embraced the *Grumble Fast*, the Lord sovereignly intervened. Conventional wisdom says a spirit of Jezebel must be confronted. Yet, as we obediently gave thanks, the Lord delivered us supernaturally and without confrontation. Suddenly, the Lord moved unexpectedly and powerfully in other situations in our city. Though dealing with the 'spirit of Jezebel' (remember it is a spirit, not a person) is more complex than thanksgiving alone, you will ***not*** overcome it unless you do shift into gratitude.[26]

In this new era, if we remain with church as usual, we will be left unprotected. The world, and especially God's people, are facing severe geographical, cultural, theological and political foes—inspired and directed by Leviathan and Jezebel spirits. Christians are facing the worst persecutions since the early Church. The Lord is calling the church to come up higher in praise and worship. It is the sound of corporate praise coming from every heart that will vaporise these giants! While in the dream it only took one bold person to inspire courage in the face of ISIS, the enemy did not leave until *every* lover of God was passionately and courageously engaged in praise and proclamation. There can be ***no*** spectators!

Yes, the enemy intimidates. But when our focus is on our deliverer, the enemy diminishes in size to us—we no longer feel like grasshoppers in the company of giants. ***And***, the enemy cannot survive in the atmosphere of gratitude and praise. The devil cannot breathe the air of heaven!

Though we are assured of the Lord's promise to deliver us from ***every*** fear, trouble and affliction, yet when our enemy is in our face and eyeballing us, we need to speak confidently. We must speak God's truth and proclaim our allegiance to the King of kings. *'With God's help we* ***will*** *prevail...And with God's help we'll trample down our* ***every*** *foe!'* (Psalm 108:13 TPT)

Whether your enemy is afflicting you in the natural, or demon hordes are attacking your mind and heart, the Lord of heaven's armies is your defender, shield and helper.

PRAYER

Spend time praising the Lord by personalising today's Scriptures.[27]

Lord God Almighty, thank You for delivering me from every enemy, seen and unseen, known and unknown. Yeshua, Lamb of God, You are worthy of all praise. Your blood has redeemed me from the power and kingdom of darkness. You triumphed over death and hell.

I lift to you my circumstances where I feel the enemy breathing down my neck and tormenting my mind with defeat. In the name of Jesus of Nazareth, and with Your help, I will prevail; I will tread down every enemy. I thank You for Your deliverance and help. I thank You that the gates of hell cannot prevail against the Messiah, the Son of the Living God. At the cross, Yeshua trampled down every enemy! I thank You, Lord, for rescuing me from every fear and foe. Amen

Keep praising Him. Declare other Scriptures about the Lord's deliverance. Continue giving the sincere 'sacrifice of thanksgiving' today.[28]

- Declare who He is—the Messiah, Deliverer, Saviour, the Son of the Living God.
- Cry out to Him: 'Hosanna—glory to God who saves us'.
- Thank Him for rescuing you—even if you can't see it yet!

---

24. 2 Chronicles 20
25. Isaiah 52:8
26. The 'spirit of Jezebel' is a big topic. The purpose of raising it here is not to teach but give testimony. Many overlook the importance of repentance and of shifting the heart from rejection and agreement with the enemy. We overcome as we give thanks for what God has done, and is doing in your life. Gratitude is an important key. If you need to research that subject check out the books in the bibliography, and go to the simple checklist in Appendix 4

    https://sidroth.org/television/tv-archives/dr-michael-brown-4/?src=banner_tv
27. Psalm 18:48-49; Psalm 50:14-15; Psalm 109:30-31; Psalm 32:7 1 Psalm 108:13; 1 Corinthians 15:57 Matthew 16:18-20
28. Psalm 27:5-14; Psalm 47:5-8; Psalm 18:16-19, 33-40; Psalm 68 : 20-26;

DAY 8

Our King Is Formidable, Invisible and Full of Glory

Today we start with the activation. Below are Scriptures that are powerful declarations of who God is. Our God is awesome. There is no-one like Him.

ACTIVATION

Read the Scriptures below slowly. Then read them aloud, deliberately and with strong conviction—like a decree.

'The Lord God Most High is astonishing, awesome beyond words! He's the formidable and powerful King over all the earth. He's the one who conquered the nations before us and placed them all under our feet.' (Psalm 47: 2-3 TPT)

'Because of this my praises rise to the King of all the universe who is indestructible, invisible, and full of glory, the only God who is worthy of the highest honors throughout all of time and throughout the eternity of eternities. Amen!' (1 Timothy 1:17 TPT)

'Blessed are You, Lord God of Israel, our Father, forever and ever. Yours, O Lord, is the greatness, The power and the glory, The victory and the majesty; For all that is in heaven

and in earth is Yours; Yours is the kingdom, O Lord, And You are exalted as head over all. Both riches and honor come from You, And You reign over all. In Your hand is power and might; In Your hand it is to make great And to give strength to all. 'Now therefore, our God, We thank You And praise Your glorious name.' (1 Chronicles 29: 11-13 NKJV)

Awe—Awesome—Fear of the Lord

The word awesome is so over-used today. It is used to describe anything from hamburgers to kind words to space technology! The real meaning of awesome is closer to the phrase 'the fear of the Lord'. Awesome actually means to 'inspire awe or dread'. The fear of the Lord is about awe, respect, reverence, or dread. These meanings also invoke the concept of worship. These connections are seen when comparing two translations of Proverbs 14:27.

*'The **fear of the Lord** is a fountain of life'. (Proverbs 14:27 NKJV)*

*'To **worship God in wonder and awe** opens a fountain of life within you.'(Proverbs 14:27 TPT)*

The Scripture ends with a beautiful promise of escaping death's domain. The fear of the Lord, being in awe of Him, worshipping Him with the respect He deserves as King of the Universe—this action protects us from death's domain!

He is the only 'formidable and powerful King' ever seen.

He is the only King over ***all*** of the earth!

He is the only King on earth who is indestructible.

He is the only King on earth who is invisible, and who has also been visible.

He is the only King on earth who is ***full*** of glory!

He is the only King on earth who is worthy of the highest honour through eternity!

Compared to our great and awesome King, what is the size of your circumstances today? To get some perspective, if you were to write one or two of your challenges alongside His description above; how do they compare?

Throughout today, return frequently to these powerful Scriptures. Go to them over and over. They are a powerful way to enter through the gates of gratitude and praise.

PRAYER

Three different ways to utilise today's Scripture in your time of gratitude prayer and praise.

1. Lift up any challenging circumstances before Him and proclaim these Scriptures. Remind your emotions and thoughts, 'This is who I worship and trust today. My King is Formidable, Indestructible, Invisible, and Full of glory!'
2. Proclaim these words to the prince powers of the air. Remind them who is fighting for you!
3. Praise Him. Use these Scriptures to give Him thanks for who He is. Use these Scriptures to praise Him.

Continue to praise Him.

DAY 9

Outwit Leviathan

'No enemy will outwit him, no wicked man overcome him.'(Psalm 89:22 CJB)

*'Bring me your true and sincere thanks... **Honor me by trusting in me in your day of trouble.**' (Psalm 50: 14-15 TPT)*

The Lord made a covenant with King David; you can read it in Psalm 89. Among the promises made to David, God promised that ***no*** enemy would be able to outwit David! The sweet psalmist of Israel, a man after God's heart, would not just be protected from his enemies, but the Lord would defeat and crush every adversary.[29]

Praising the Lord, especially in the face of adversity or while eyeballing an enemy, brings great honour to the Lord. Such worship is an expression of trusting in Him. It will also deliver us from strong enemies—even Leviathan.

Leviathan—Creature and Symbol[30]

Though created as a natural creature[31], Scripture most often speaks of Leviathan[32] as a symbol of the serpent, dragon, crocodile[33], Egypt and Babylon.[34] It is a major demonic water spirit.

'The Crocodile Hunter', namely the late Steve Irwin, brought international attention to Australia's saltwater crocodiles. Mainly found in northern Australia, we Aussies call them 'salties'—and they are not to be messed with! Most people killed by crocodiles have naively (or stupidly) strayed into their habitat. Unless you have the skills of Steve Irwin, the best way to outwit this vicious reptile is to stay out of its habitat! If you do get caught, a few brave or desperate souls have escaped by poking it in the eyes!

Job warns not to take on Leviathan[35]. God alone can deal with it.[36] But we can and should avoid its habitat.

Mouth

The body of the crocodile is two-thirds teeth and mouth! This creature takes its prey in the mouth, and then using its tail to twist and turn in a downward spiral, it drowns its victim. Twisted and defiling communications are a sign of Leviathan at work. As a serpent, Leviathan twists and bites to deceive and poison. As a dragon, this principality seeks to accuse and discredit.[37] The expertise of each of these symbolic creatures align perfectly with the devil, who is a murderer and the father of lies.[38]

James warns us about our mouths—specifically our tongue. It is a fire that cannot be tamed and full of toxic poison.[39] Leviathan, as the demonic serpent, seduces to entwine our tongue in his evil purposes.

The assignment of twisted communications is to tear truth to pieces, and with it, reputation, relationship and destiny. If we comply and agree with it, Leviathan wins. To outwit this demonic tempter, we have to break agreement with its mouth and invite the Spirit of God to cleanse our heart and lips. By speaking, praying and singing in Holy Spirit tongues, our human tongues are infused with heavenly communications—His love and truth! Hence, the *Grumble Fast* is powerful to deliver.

Honour or Dishonour

Life and death are in the power of the tongue. Words of life honour God, ourselves and others. Honour attributes value to a person. Songs of praise are expressions of how much we value the Lord. Conversely, Leviathan tempts our tongue to dishonour and devalue God, ourselves, and each other. 'With our tongues we praise our Lord and Father. Yet, with the same tongues we curse people, who were created in God's likeness' (James 3:9 GW).

Grumbling and Dishonour Activate Leviathan

In despair and self-pity, Job cursed the day of his birth (Job 3:1). According to Psalm 139, our birthday and each day of our life are watched over and recorded by the Lord. To curse our birthday is an insult to the Lord's plan and destiny for our life. When Job cursed his birthday, it not only dishonoured the Lord but ***activated*** the demonic principality called Leviathan. (Job 8:3)[40] Do you struggle to celebrate your birthday? Ask the Lord if this is a key for you.

Israel fell for the devil's lies regarding their destiny; '*It would have been better for us to serve the Egyptians than that we should die in the wilderness*'. But God had promised Israel their own land, filled with milk and honey. When we grumble, complain and find fault—we come into agreement with the devil's lies. When we believe lies and accusations, our destiny can be drowned by the death-roll of the demonic crocodile.

Grumbling may activate Leviathan, but gratitude, praise and trusting God remove us from its habitat. When we stop speaking its language, we are freed from its destructive plans. Giving thanks, especially in our day of trouble, is faith in action and enables us to outwit the entrapment of Leviathan.

Levi and Leviathan

Anne Hamilton eloquently identifies the link between Levi and Leviathan;

> It's no coincidence that Levi and Leviathan start with the same letters. Their functions are similar: the tribe of Levi to serve in the Tabernacle and Temple; Leviathan to serve - originally - in God's court. Because the gifts of God are irrevocable, the fallen spirit Leviathan still has an office as a guardian of honour.
>
> It's also a guardian of the threshold...
>
> I have always found that, if you are beset by Leviathan, the issue is one of honour. If we are not allowed to dishonour even the fallen angels (see 2 Peter 2 and Jude 1), why should we be allowed to dishonour any part of creation - including ourselves? Leviathan is 'a spirit of the deep, a spirit of the threshold, a spirit of backlash and a spirit concerned with honour.'[41]

The word '*Levi*' means to be attached. The history and call of the tribe of Levi is about being attached to God, giving Him honour. The tribe of Levi were the only ones who stood with

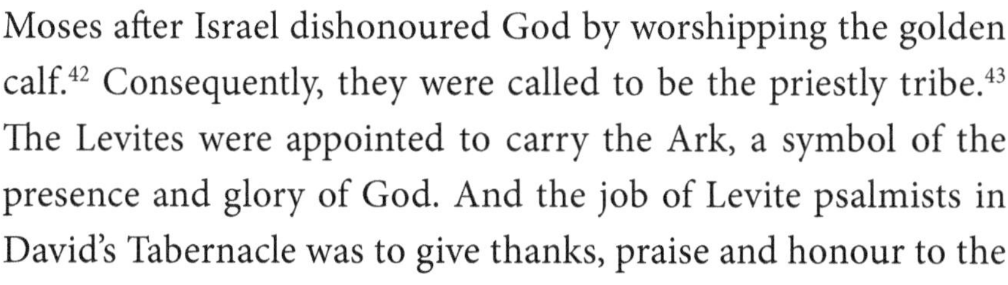

Moses after Israel dishonoured God by worshipping the golden calf.[42] Consequently, they were called to be the priestly tribe.[43] The Levites were appointed to carry the Ark, a symbol of the presence and glory of God. And the job of Levite psalmists in David's Tabernacle was to give thanks, praise and honour to the Lord.[44]

Conversely, Leviathan 'detaches' itself from God by dishonouring Him. Lucifer, heaven's original worship leader, detached himself through rebellion and pride. The scheme of Leviathan is to get you and me to 'detach' ourselves from God by proudly grumbling.

In our day of trouble, we have a choice—to praise or grumble. Our choice will reveal how much, or how little, we value the Lord, His truth and His promises.

ACTIVATION

Leviathan is the king of pride and resists the breath of God.[45] We overcome pride with humility. Surrender, repentance, prayer and worship are all acts of humility. Take time today to:

1. Bow and surrender before His throne.
2. Invite Holy Spirit to show you any pride to repent of.
3. Receive the breath of Holy Spirit.
4. Release gratitude to God. Sing songs of praise and activate the frequencies of the glory! (2 Chronicles 5:13)

PRAYER

Righteous and loving Father, throughout this day, let the words of my mouth and the meditation of my heart be acceptable in Your sight. You are my strength and my Redeemer.[46] Amen

Continue to pray and sing in tongues—the language of heaven. Then, reflect and record in your journal:

- Answers from Holy Spirit to problems for today
- A noticeable shift or change in your heart as you prayed or sang in tongues, especially any changes you noticed in your heart toward circumstances or people.

---

29. See Appendix 4 Checklist of Leviathan and Jezebel
30. Psalm 104:26
31. Strongs H 3882 livyathan = serpent, crocodile, mourning, figurative of constellation of dragon, symbol of Babylon. From root H 3867 *lava* = to wine, union
32. Isaiah 27:1
33. Lance Wallnau: Breaking Free Leviathan mp3 Part one & Part 2
34. Job 41:1-8
35. Isaiah 27:1
36. Revelation 12:9,10
37. John 8:44
38. James 3:8-10
39. Job 3:8 'May those curse it who curse the day, Those who are ready to arouse Leviathan.'
41. Anne Hamilton Facebook post 23/8/2016: https://www.facebook.com/photo.php?fbid=1096973943683878&set=a.994100490637891&type=3&theater
42. Exodus 32:26
43. Exodus 32:29
44. 1 Chronicles 16:4
45. Job 41:34, 16
46. Psalm 19:14

DAY 10

God Is Good

'Oh, give thanks to the Lord, for He is good!' (Psalm 118:1; 136:1-4 NKJV)

'For You are my God; Your Spirit is good.' (Psalm 143:10 NKJV)

'The goodness of God endures continually.' (Psalm 52:1 NKJV)

'No one is good but One, that is, God.' (Matthew 19:17 NKJV)

'Oh, that men would give thanks to the Lord for His goodness' (Psalm 107:8 NKJV)

'And [Moses] said, 'Please, show me Your glory.' Then He [God] said, 'I will make all My goodness pass before you, and I will proclaim the name of the Lord before you.' (Exodus 33:18,19 NKJV)

Begin today by declaring these Scriptures aloud—with thanksgiving!

The Psalmist calls us to give thanks because God is good—forever! His goodness never fluctuates or changes. God's goodness is reliable and wonderful.

> *'He is the rock, His work is perfect; for all His ways are justice, a God of truth and without injustice; Righteous and upright is He.' (Deuteronomy 32: 4 NKJV)*

As the Chris Tomlin song says; 'You're a good, good father... It's who you are...You are perfect in all of Your ways...'[47]

Life can be tough, full of challenges and traumas, but His goodness remains steadfast. His goodness is not diminished or impacted by our circumstances. In the midst of our worst trouble, we can still give thanks because God is *always* good. His goodness remains immovable and trustworthy. What a comfort when our life is crumbling or hard to fathom!

Everything God does is good. At creation; *'God saw everything that He had made, and indeed it was very **good**.'* (Genesis 1:31 NKJV)

With the change and overuse of language, the word *good* can feel like God is ordinary. Especially when we use words like 'awesome' and 'cool' to describe things as basic as hamburgers. Everything we 'like' seems to get these accolades. So, we think something that is described as 'good' has to be mediocre in comparison to what is 'awesome' or 'excellent'. Yet the dictionary says good is: *morally excellent, virtuous, righteous, pious, of high quality, and excellent.*

God is good and what He does is good. Perhaps awesome should be kept for those things that really are 'good'! We should keep our best words for the Lord's character and nature—after all, there is no-one else like Him! He is above every other name.

It is a horrible thing to consider, but recently I momentarily pondered what it would be like if God were evil. Thankfully, this will ***never*** be true. As I contemplated the unthinkable, I realised, if it were true, we would not be here! History shows that evil regimes trash, plunder, kill and create havoc. Evil cannot create. Evil cannot love. Evil cannot redeem. Anything that was in existence would quickly be destroyed because lies and murder seek to eliminate anything good.

Therefore, do not doubt—God ***is*** good! Everything He does is good. Everything about Him is good. Creation reflects His goodness and beauty. His greatest demonstration of goodness was sending His only Son to earth, to remove the power of sin and death.

Goodness and Glory

Moses asked to see the LORD's glory. He saw God's goodness. The glory or, *kabod,* that Moses asked to see, is the weight, splendour and fullness of God's face or countenance. God said to Moses; *'I will make all* ***My goodness*** *pass before you, and I will proclaim the name of the Lord before you.'* (Exodus 33:18,19 NKJV)

Moses was shown goodness; the perfection of God's character—the beauty of right actions, fairness, mercy, enabling prosperity, gladness, welfare. Moses would get to hear the Lord's name pronounced. Moses was not allowed to see the face of God, the glory, but he did see His back, or His goodness. Like two sides of a coin, Romans 11:22 tells God's people to consider both His 'goodness and severity'. The *Easton Dictionary* sums up God's goodness as 'giving and forgiving'.

When Goodness Is Questioned

Despite the goodness of God, since the Garden of Eden, the devil has sought to convince the sons of Adam that God is not good and His Word not trustworthy. Like Adam and Eve, we have all been tempted to question God's goodness.

As the end-times roll on, the devil's efforts only increase in quantity and intensity. He bombards the saints to wear us down. His deceptions are like chocolates laced with poison. He baits us with offence and misunderstanding. He twists and distorts truth until we believe a lie.

Anytime we are lured and swallow the bait, we end up grumbling. In the midst of the bombardment of life, it is too easy to forget God is good. The devil uses our painful circumstances to cause us to doubt the goodness of God. But the fact remains; God is good and there is ***not*** one grain of evil in Him.

Your circumstances cannot change God nor His goodness. But God's goodness can change you, your attitude and even your circumstances!

ACTIVATION

1. Meditate on, and contemplate, the Lord's goodness to you in the last week. Write down three experiences. Now thank Him for His goodness.
2. Play the song: 'Good, Good Father' (or your own favourite song) and thank Him for His goodness penetrating your circumstances today.[48]
3. Personalise and declare aloud the Scriptures at the start of today's devotional and place them over your circumstances.
4. Ask Holy Spirit to show you any circumstance where the devil convinced you that God is not good. Spend time before the Lord to pray through any areas of doubting God's goodness.

PRAYER

Lord God Almighty, You are good and Your mercies are new every morning. I am so grateful that there is no evil within You. I am so grateful that everything you do is beautiful and flows from Your goodness. (Psalm 119:68 TPT)

As I lift my circumstances to You today, I declare the truth; You are good.

I confess there are times I have believed the lies of the enemy. I repent of believing the lies that you are not good. I break agreement with the lies of the devil. Thank-you that the blood of Jesus cleanses my heart, my emotions, my memories, and my thoughts. As You did for Moses, let Your goodness pass before me, overshadow me, and inspire me with hope today. Amen.

---

47. 'Good Good Father'. Lyrics by Tony Brown, Pat Barrett

48. YouTube is a great option for listening to free worship music: https://www.youtube.com/watch?v=CqybaIesbuA

DAY 11

If You're Breathing—Join the Symphony of Praise

> *'Let everything that has breath praise the Lord. Praise the Lord!' (Psalm 150 NKJV)*

Today you qualify to join the symphony of praise. You are obviously breathing if you are reading this! And as long as we have breath, we are called to praise. There is no-one alive who is not called to give praise to the King of glory! So today, if you are alive, you qualify. And those who are dead in Christ will be praising Him in heavenly places for eternity!

The call to praise is not limited to human beings, it also goes out to ***all*** of creation.

> *'Praise him, all beasts and birds, mice and men, kings, queens, princes, and princesses, young men and maidens, children and babes, old and young alike, everyone everywhere! Let them all join in with this orchestra of praise. For the name of the Lord is the only name we raise! His stunning splendor ascends higher than the heavens. He anoints his people with strength and authority, showing his great*

favor to all his godly lovers, even to his princely people, Israel, who are so close to his heart. Hallelujah! Praise the Lord!' (Psalm 148:10-14 TPT)

While writing and rehearsing the song 'All Your Works Shall Praise'[49], a chorus of native birds in the trees outside our lounge room would erupt into song with me. I was so aware of 'All Creation' giving Him praise.

Just after our ministry concluded our *Grumble Fast* in 2018, a visiting ministry was in town on a prayer assignment. While out on-site and seeking the Lord where He specifically wanted us to pray, all of a sudden, a magpie showed up. The magpie is an Australian native song-bird. While it may seem bizarre, the magpie sat on my car until we 'got the message' as to where the Lord wanted us to pray. Since then, we regularly have had some 14-20 magpies outside our home singing their songs of praise!

All of creation was meant to be a choir of praises. All of earth was meant to be a worship centre. Jesus said that if we won't praise Him, He would call for the rocks to praise. (Luke 19:38-40 NKJV) Prior to this, the people had been singing and yelling out, "Blessed is the King who comes in the name of the Lord!' Peace in heaven and glory in the highest!' The passage in Matthew 21:9 (NKJV) says, '*Hosanna to the Son of David!*' Hosanna literally means 'save us, deliver us'. It is a cry of recognition of the Messiah—glory to God who saves us—the redeemer of the lineage of David!

The religious people got upset. They were upset that Yeshua was being recognized as the Messiah! They were upset that the people were worshipping Yeshua as their deliverer—and they were upset the worship was loud and public! Jesus responded, 'I tell you that if these should keep silent, the stones would immediately cry out.'

Heaven and earth declare Yeshua is Messiah; He is the deliverer, He is the King of kings, and He is to be honoured and worshipped. If we keep quiet, if we do not agree with heaven's decree, if we are not willing to give the King of glory the praise due to His name—He can easily find another source!

Let us not leave His praise to compacted stones! That might sound like a weird statement. But Adam, —Mankind—, was created from dirt. Believers in Jesus are called 'living stones'. If we refuse to give Him praise, it is not hard for Him to create or find another living stone that is willing to praise Him! But we would miss out on the blessing. Praise is the environment, the air and the power of heaven!

The symphony of praise is a call from heaven to earth. No person and no creature is excluded. We were created to praise. We were created to worship our maker. The worship of heaven is a praise orchestra. If you are breathing—join the orchestra of praise!

ACTIVATION

1. Commit to joining the symphony of praise!
2. Grab hold of your musical instrument, and/or grab a worship CD and spend time in praise.
3. The Psalms were written as songs. In your own way, try singing Psalm 148, Psalm 150.
4. Observe and write down any noticeable changes to your environment, within your heart, or in clarity of hearing Holy Spirit.

PRAYER

Thank You, Father, for the breath in me to give You praise. Thank You for creating me with the ability and desire to praise You. Thank You for the privilege of honouring You with praise today. I agree with heaven and affirm who You are—Messiah, Deliverer, King of kings.

Thank You that my voice of praise is not in isolation, but each time I praise You I connect with the sound created by other worshippers on earth, I connect with heaven, and I connect with creation in the orchestra and choir of praise.

Thank You for the anointing of strength and authority that rests on me as I join Your praise symphony. Amen

Keep praising Him as you read through Revelation 5:11-13.

---

49. Based on Psalm 145:10-13, "All Your Works" © 2012 Ruth Webb

    Track one: "Gardens of Love" (Instrumental) Digital Download https://www.tabernacleofdavid.org.au/shop/cd-29/gardens-of-love-digital-download.html

    Disc one, Track two: "Welcome King of Glory" (Worship Team) Digital Downloadhttps://www.tabernacleofdavid.org.au/shop/cd-29/welcome-king-of-glory-digital-download.html

DAY 12

In Everything Give Thanks

*'**In everything give thanks;** for this is the will of God.' (1 Thessalonians 5:18 NKJV)*

*'Be anxious for nothing, but **in everything** by prayer and supplication, **with thanksgiving,** let your requests be made known to God.' (Philippians 4:6 NKJV)*

'Giving thanks always for all things...' (Ephesians 5:20 NKJV)

When life is going well, it is relatively easy to give thanks. Even Israel broke into singing, dancing, and celebration when delivered from the Egyptians. But what about when life throws you a curve ball? What about times of great disappointment, injustice, trauma, tragedy and loss?

The dilemma for the human soul is how to give thanks when life is tough. As Christians we know gratitude is what God wants from us, but sometimes it's difficult to do. Herein lies the tension of our struggle. We want to obey and give thanks, but when life is tough or unfair, we can't help ourselves from grumbling. Many also struggle with the idea that giving thanks 'for' everything doesn't seem fair.

A few key points to remember about this instruction to be grateful:

1. 1 Thessalonians 5:18 says; give thanks 'in', not 'for'. *The Passion Translation* says, '*I**n** the midst of **everything**—always* give thanks.' Ephesians 5:20 speaks of '***for all things***.' But *The Passion Translation* renders that verse as all 'people' rather than all 'things'.[50] If you are struggling to give thanks ***for*** the chaos, then ***begin*** with giving thanks ***in*** the middle of the chaos. Give thanks because He is with you in the midst of the storm.

2. The Lord does ***not*** ask us to deny our pain or suffering. Rather, in giving thanks, we acknowledge our tough reality, but simultaneously, that our trust is in the Lord—His strength and His answers.

3. The Lord does not ask us to excuse injustice or unrighteous acts. Righteousness and justice are the foundation of His throne. Again, thanksgiving in the face of injustice is not denial but rather our acknowledgment that we trust in Him to give us strength to walk through the fire, and for His justice to eventually prevail. He will have the last Word!

4. The Lord *is* asking us to come to Him with the reality of our pain. He is asking us to remember Him in the midst of ***all*** our circumstances. Gratitude is about our perception and attitude towards God—in the midst of victory or trial. Whether life is great or chaotic, thanksgiving remembers Him.

Compare God to Your Tough Circumstances

Ask these questions to see if your circumstances have impacted God:

1. Have your circumstances caused God Himself to change? No. He remains righteous and loving.
2. Have your circumstances caused God's Word to change? No. He remains faithful to His Word.
3. Can God help you through the situation? Absolutely!

> *'We all experience times of testing, which is normal for every human being.* ***But God*** *will be faithful to you... each test is an opportunity to trust him more, for ...God has provided for you a way of escape that will bring you out of it victoriously.' (1 Corinthians 10:13 TPT)*

Underneath much of our resistance to give thanks in the midst of loss, is the belief that God could have, but did not, prevent our tragic loss. *Where was God? 'Why' has this happened? 'Why' did He not prevent it? Does He really love me? Did God really say? 'Where' is my miracle?* All these questions are reminiscent of the snake in the Garden of Eden.

The human soul wants the *why* question answered before we give thanks. But God asks us to give thanks first, before we know the answer to *why*. Thanksgiving is a step of faith. Our basic trust in God is tested—even to the very core of our being. Sometimes this test derails us, even tipping us into bitterness and unbelief.

Remember Israel's slavery in Egypt? The Egyptians treated Israel harshly because they were afraid of them. In the midst of their pain, Moses showed up with a word from God. Moses assured them; 'God has heard your cry for help. He is bringing you out of Egypt's tyranny.' Now that should have been good news, right? No. Israel wouldn't listen to Moses, because, '*they were so* ***discouraged****, and their* ***slavery was so cruel.***' (Exodus 6:5-9 CJB)

Any time we have been really crushed by life and someone offers a prophecy of hope, our heart can react similarly—the promise is too good to be true, and the despondent response is,'Oh, yeah?!' I know I have reacted this way—until getting a swift reminder to give thanks.

It may seem hard to believe, but when our heavenly Father asks us to give thanks in the midst of *everything, He* is actually offering a loving ***gift***. It is a divine strategy. Thanksgiving provides wind beneath our wings. It helps us be like eagles— to soar above storms. By contrast, grumbling causes us to crash and be pummelled by grief and hopelessness.

Gratitude is the oxygen of heaven, enabling us to breathe during trouble. Praise and thanksgiving are the language of heaven—so we can invite Him into our circumstances. Grumbling causes our eyes to be fixed downward on our circumstances. Gratitude sets our eyes on Him and hence, we know 'How Great is our God'.

Jesus, '*Having disarmed principalities and powers, He made a public spectacle of them,* ***triumphing*** *over them* ***in it***.' (Colossians 2:15 NKJV) He overcame death in the midst of being 'in it'!

Giving thanks '*in the midst of everything*' protects our heart and our faith. It keeps us in truth. Gratitude positions our heart to receive His supernatural help and victory.

ACTIVATION

1. Find a worship song to help fix your thoughts on His greatness.
2. Find a Psalm that best describes where you are at today—let it minister deeply.
3. Pray in the Spirit.
4. Settle your heart in His Presence. Try to snuggle into Him and pour out your burden.

PRAYER

Holy and Righteous Father, I am so grateful Your ways are above my ways and Your thoughts are above my thoughts. When my heart is overwhelmed, I run to You, the rock of my salvation. You are a strong tower. In the times of trouble, I can run to You and be safe. I thank You that there is comfort and protection under Your wings. I am so grateful You are not diminished or weakened by my circumstances. Despite what I face, Your Word remains intact. You are holy, You are Lord God Almighty, Creator of heaven and earth. I praise Your holy name. Amen

Continue to praise Him.

---

50. Ephesians 5:20 from *The Passion Translation* is discussed at length on Day 36 and Day 37 as we consider giving thanks for the people in our life.

DAY 13

Nothing too Hard for the Creator!

'Adonai Yahweh, you made heaven and earth by your great strength and powerful arm. ***Nothing*** *is too hard for you.' (Jeremiah 32:17 GW)*

'The earth was without form, and void; and darkness was on the face of the deep. And the Spirit of God was hovering over the face of the waters.' (Genesis 1:2 NKJV)

The Bible is filled with miracles; from the creation in Genesis to the countless miracles of Jesus and the early church. Jeremiah reminds us, if God can make the heavens and earth from nothing, then any problem on earth is not too hard for the Creator!

Jeremiah was prophesying about captivity in Babylon. The Lord had said Israel would be freed after 70 years. Jeremiah was told to do a prophetic act (i.e., acting out the prophetic word). Jeremiah had to buy land in readiness for their freedom! After receiving the title deeds for the land, Jeremiah reminded himself and Israel of God's power and greatness. Though the circumstances in Babylon looked hopeless, if God could create heaven and earth, and if He was able to get Israel out of Egypt, couldn't He also rescue Israel out of Babylon? God was well ***able*** to do what He had promised.

When life is tough, it is good to rehearse what He has ***already*** done. Remember what He did at creation and remember what He did for Israel. And consider all the miracles in the Bible. Sarah, Hannah, Elizabeth and Mary had babies supernaturally. God stopped the hungry lions' mouths for Daniel. The sun stopped still for Joshua. Lazarus and Jesus rose from the dead. The miracles of Jesus were so many and varied that John said the whole world could not contain all the books needed to record all the testimonies! (John 21:25)

In modern times, the establishment of Israel as a nation in 1948, and then the 6-day war of 1967, were definitely miracle after miracle. Interestingly, after Israel became a nation in 1948, healing ministries broke out in the Church across the globe. Miracles are happening in the Church today akin to the early church. Yet, many still ask, where are the miracles today?

I thought I had finished writing this book when the Lord gave me a challenging download. I had been asking the Lord about miracles today and the issues of doubt vs faith we all often face.

He reminded me of the miracles throughout the Bible from Genesis to Revelation. We believe it for Israel, for Abraham, Joshua, Paul and others, '*but what about me*?' We may ask. We believe but don't believe. So, I prayed: 'Lord, I believe, help my unbelief'.

Then He showed me I had first learned about the Biblical miracles in Sunday School. They were taught as amazing stories. The

Lord showed me I had absorbed these stories in a way not much different to 'fairy tales'. They were not personal for 'me'. They were remote, confined to some distant history or geographical region. When situations arise and we need to grasp the possibility of miracles for ourselves, how do we respond? On one level we believe the historical accounts as miracles. But on a subconscious level, have we evaluated Biblical miracles merely as 'fairy tales' and myths, and thus make it harder for us to really believe for a miracle?

I had the sense the Lord is saying that if we absorb Biblical miracles as reality, rather than fantasy, we could more easily say with Jeremiah, '*You made heaven and earth by Your great strength and powerful arm. Nothing is too hard for You.*' (Jeremiah 32:17 GW)

Now, think back and remember—what has God done for you throughout your life? What unseen miracles has He done for you to protect and provide?

Genesis 1:2 describes a place of darkness and chaos over which the Spirit of God brooded and lingered over—something like a mother hen sitting on something ready to be birthed. The breath of God moved over the chaos. Movement is the beginning of sound. And then God spoke, or rather, sung the Word!

Is there any darkness or chaos in your circumstances that you are lifting to Him today? Allow the breath of God to brood and breathe over it. Invite the Holy Spirit to breathe, stir and move over any confusion and disorder. Release the sound of Him moving and hovering over you.

Let His Word and His light be released into your darkness and your chaos: 'Let there be light'! (Genesis 1:3 NKJV)

ACTIVATION

1. Contemplate and meditate on His power and His creative miracles. Let faith arise.
2. Consider your circumstances today, and now compare them to the power and creativity of God. Lift your circumstances to Him.

PRAYER

Lord God Almighty, You are the Creator of the Universe. By Your great strength and power, You made all things. I am so grateful that nothing in my life is too difficult for You! You are greater, bigger and more powerful than every circumstance I face.

I repent of those places and times I have considered Your miracles as myths, fairy tales or only available to Israel or super Christians. Cleanse my heart and mind from every lie. I acknowledge You are the Creator of heaven and earth. And You are able to perform the words You have spoken to me. Amen

Continue to praise Him. Nothing you face is beyond His power or creativity.

Thank Him for His creative power penetrating your circumstances.

DAY 14

Gratitude and End-Time Survival

*'In the final days the culture of society will become extremely fierce and difficult for the people of God...They will be **ungrateful** and ungodly.' (2 Timothy 3:1-2 TPT)*

'Do everything without grumbling or arguing, so that you might be blameless and innocent, children of God in the midst of a crooked and twisted generation. Among them you shine as lights in the world...' (Philippians 2:14-15 TLV)

In the Middle East today, believers are driven from their homes, kidnapped, abused, raped and beheaded by terrorists. Current worldwide figures show that Christians are the most persecuted group in the world; 11 Christians *per day* are being murdered for their faith!

In the West, persecution comes by psychological and illogical political correctness. During the 2019 Australian Election, rugby star Israel Folau lost his $4 million contract because he quoted a Bible verse on social media. The Biblical quote spoke of those who would go to hell. PM Scott Morrison, a Pentecostal Christian, was hounded to see if he too believed in hell—as part of the political debate! And when he miraculously won the election—pundits were shocked to discover that many Australians were afraid of losing their religious freedoms!

The hatred toward Christians is part of the end-time spirit. Jesus warned us, if they hated Him, they will hate us too! Such vitriolic hatred tests a person's commitment and gratitude to the Lord.

Paul warned us it would get difficult for believers in the last days. He also identified that gratitude would diminish in the end-times. In other words, grumbling would increase and be one of the signposts of the end-times!

Demonic strongholds are entrenched and empowered by grumbling, therefore as darkness increases, so too will grumbling. End-times issues will test our resolve to give thanks rather than grumble! Developing a lifestyle of gratitude will be necessary for remaining faithful to the Lord in the midst of persecution. Thanksgiving and worship in the glory realms will be necessary for overcoming victory.

The one distinguishing difference in the end-times is light and darkness. Those bound by darkness will grumble and those walking in the light will praise. Therefore, we really need to secure the concept and habit of gratitude.

The end-time spirit of ingratitude has a focus upon self and entitlements; i.e., selfishness. Rick Joyner had two visions described in his books *Fire on the Mountain* and *The Valley.* In the second book, *The Valley*, Joyner[51] says selfishness will be deadly for believers in the end-times. Believers operating in selfishness will have no defence against the enemy.

Selfishness has an expectation to be pampered and given entitlements. If these are withheld, one can expect toddler-like behaviour. Selfishness is the antithesis of dying to self. So too, grumbling is the antithesis to thanksgiving.

DAY 14

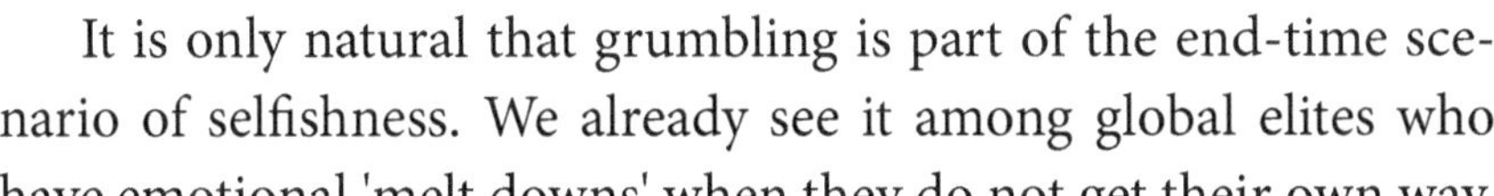

It is only natural that grumbling is part of the end-time scenario of selfishness. We already see it among global elites who have emotional 'melt downs' when they do not get their own way.

The only way to overcome this end-time spirit of selfishness and grumbling is the way of the cross and in gratitude expressed to the Lamb who was slain. Yeshua's defeat of all the devil's works include selfishness and grumbling. The cross is the power of God to overcome the end-time spirit.

Grumbling caused a generation of Israelites to die in the wilderness and never reach the Promised Land. Later, grumbling led to rebellion, idolatry and further captivity, but this time in Babylon. Grumbling basically says God can't or won't help me. When we limit God from helping us, we effectively invite the devil to 'help' us instead! Therefore, if we are seduced to grumble, we can be captured by the end-time spirit.

Israel could not sing the song of the Lord while they were captives in Babylon. The song of the Lord is not a natural sound in the devil's lair! Mystery Babylon itself has its own unique sound—and it's not praise! It is a sound of rebellion, hatred and murder; being 'drunk with…the blood of the martyrs of Jesus.' (Revelation 17:6 NKJV)

In the book of Revelation, all who are with the Lamb fill the air with praise 24/7. And 'Mystery Babylon' wars against the Lamb and all who are with Him. (Revelation 17:14) I believe strongly the end-time battle is like a 'battle of the bands'—it is over who we worship, and our sounds and songs of praise. When Babylon is defeated, its deathly music and sounds will also be silenced! (Revelation 17:22)

Praise is the language, environment and power of heaven. In heaven the Lamb is honoured 24/7, and His name and power are exalted. The sound begins in the heart of gratitude. Therefore, gratitude and praise in our homes are like a welcome mat for heaven to enter our earthly neighbourhoods.

However, grumbling is the language, environment and power of hell. Grumbling is an invitation to the hordes of hell.

Israel overcame giants and enemies when they went out in praise! So too, gratitude is a major weapon to overcome the end-time spirit of anti-Christ and Babylon.

ACTIVATION

1. Pray in tongues.
2. Confess and repent of any grumbling, complaining, ingratitude. Be as specific and thorough as possible, rather than just saying a general prayer. (1 Peter 2:9)
3. Confess to a friend according to James 5 where there is a promise of healing.
4. Ask Holy Spirit for His help to stop grumbling. Thank Him for answered prayer.

PRAYER

Father, I thank You for Your exhortation and warning of the importance of thanksgiving and praise in these end-times. I am so grateful You have not left me to fall into the trap of grumbling, but rather You have forewarned me and provided me with help to overcome. Amen

Now invite the Spirit of praise...

---

51. Rick Joyner: *Fire on the Mountain Book 2, The Valley*

DAY 15

He Never Changes

'For I am the Lord, I do not change...' (Malachi 3:6 NKJV)

'Jesus Christ is the same yesterday, today, and forever.' (Hebrews 13:8 NKJV)

'Looking unto Jesus, the author and finisher (perfecter) of our faith...' Hebrews 12:2 (NKJV)

Fashions change, seasons change, calendars change, governments change, and even language can change over time. Careers, geographical addresses and relationships may also change. Technology is changing so rapidly, and with it, communications and culture. It is suggested that technology now doubles every 12 hours! No wonder it is exceeding our ability to adapt.

There is only one constant in our world—the character of God. He *never* changes! His character is not pressured by circumstances, mood swings, or cataclysmic events on earth! He may speak to us in different ways; His strategies may vary; but His character does not shift or change. He is consistent in everything He does. All of His covenants, plans, and promises are stable and consistent because His character never changes. He is always good. He is always holy and righteous. He is always love.

He is always kind. He is always faithful. He is always truth. He is always merciful. He is always disturbed by injustice, lies, loss of innocent blood, rebellion and witchcraft.

His Character Is Biblically Consistent

God's character is consistent from Genesis to Revelation, even though some wrongly consider the 'God of the Old Testament' to be somehow different from 'God in the New Testament.' Some see Him as angry in the Old Testament and suddenly loving in the New Testament. This is erroneous. Father displays love in the Old Testament and Jesus displayed anger in the New Testament. If you look, you will find Jesus all through the Old Testament. There is only One God, not two. He is not schizophrenic, and He never changes!

Jesus said to Phillip, '*He who has seen Me has seen the Father*'(John 14:9 NKJV). Here are just four examples of the consistency of God's nature.

- 'God is love': this is found in both Old and New Testaments. (Jeremiah 31:3 John 3:16) Yeshua reveals the love of the Father to mankind.
- God of mercy is foundational to both covenants. The Ark of the Covenant is also called the 'mercy seat.' (Psalm 136:26 Psalm 145:8 Ephesians 2:4 Hebrews 4:16)
- God is Holy, and His requirement for us to also be holy is written in both covenants. (Leviticus 19:2; 1 Peter 1:16)
- God of justice is found in both covenants. He is just, justice is the foundation of His throne, and from there He executes judgement. (Psalm 82:3 Proverbs 21:3 John 5:22-30 2 Corinthians 5:10 Hebrews 12:23)

Change and Stress

Many find change difficult and uncomfortable. It is often stressful—especially the transition part where you feel you are in 'no man's land'. It is said the three most stressful changes in life are:

1. Loss of spouse or children
2. Shifting house
3. Loss or change of job

One well-known stressful transition is a woman giving birth. The final birthing process is aptly called transition! Not only is it physically demanding and painful, but the woman's body is shifting from pregnancy to having a dependent newborn.

Pain, confusion and distress are all hallmarks of severe change. Our world is becoming increasingly unstable—in the natural, culturally, politically and spiritually. With more and more sudden changes, knowing that God never changes is a profound stabiliser. His reliability provides assurance and comfort. In a world where morality is subjective and confusing, God's clear definition of sin and righteousness brings clarity to a foggy world. In the midst of our stresses it is comforting to know the One who never changes. And He is the One who has every detail in hand from beginning to end.

Past, Present and Future

'I am the Alpha and the Omega, the Beginning and the End,' says the Lord, 'who is and who was and who is to come, the Almighty.' (Revelation 1:8 NKJV)

'Looking unto Jesus, the author and finisher (perfecter) of our faith, who for the joy that was set before Him

endured the cross... and has sat down at the right hand of the throne of God.' (Hebrews 12:2 NKJV)

God Never changes.

The first struggle of transition is because the parameters of the past that we have known so well are now gone. But our present is only filled with speculation, unknowns and fear, because the future hasn't arrived yet!

In the midst of transition, we have the reassurance; God has been with us in the past and will be with us today and in the future. We can trust Him. He will not leave us or abandon us in the midst of change. He initiates both the beginning and the end of our faith journey with Him. *The Passion Translation* renders Hebrews 12:2: '*We look away* ***from the natural realm*** *and we* ***fasten our gaze onto Jesus*** *who birthed faith within us and who leads us forward into faith's perfection.*'

When we face rapidly changing and challenging circumstances, we must look away from what we see in the natural realm and fix our eyes on Jesus. Knowing God was in control of the past means we can trust Him again with our present and our future. We can lean on His stable character to receive the comfort and assuredness needed in seasons of change. He is the plumb line to measure up to, as we are transformed into His image, from glory to glory. He births our walk with Him, and He brings us into maturity.

How stressed we get during seasons of change may be linked to how much or how little we are able to trust Him. A key to reduce stress is to give thanks. Take that action today.

ACTIVATION

Are you or a loved one going through a stressful major change?

1. Give thanks—the Lord never changes! Thank Him—His shalom is stabilising you between your past, present and future. Give thanks—His goodness and righteousness are reliable and eternal. Give Him thanks —His unchanging nature is giving you comfort and assurance. Thank Him— His will and purposes are unfolding for your future.
2. Ask the Lord for a fresh revelation of the aspect of His character that is most needed by you or loved ones walking through the stressful transition. (Review the short list in paragraph two today.)
3. Write down or speak out the specific circumstances where change is stressful. Now lift these situations to the throne of grace and pray...

PRAYER

Thank you, Abba; You are reliable, You are dependable. You don't change. Even though the end result of the circumstance in my life may be unpredictable, and I may fear what the conclusion looks like, yet I can rely and depend on You today. Your steadfast and unchanging goodness, love and mercy are holding me up. You provide me with assurance and peace. You hold my past, my present and my future. Amen

Now continue to speak to Him from your heart.

DAY 16

Accepted—Not Rejected!

*'And **He chose us** to be **His very own,** joining us to himself even before he laid the foundation of the universe! **Because of His great love,** He ordained us, so that **we would be seen as holy** in his eyes with an **unstained innocence.** For it was always in **His perfect plan to adopt us as his delightful children,** through our union with Jesus, the Anointed One...' (Ephesians 1:4-6 TPT)*

Rejection is one of the most common, yet painful and debilitating conditions known to man—and one of the most difficult to overcome. There was a time I could not bring myself to even say the word, *rejection,* let alone let God deal with it!

Grumbling and rejection are best mates—joined at the hip. Grumbling and rejection are prominent in our conflict between the flesh and the spirit. The enemy mercilessly exploits rejection to divide and weaken the Church.

We were made for love. We are wired for love. We were not created for the sorrow of feeling unwanted. When God first made us '***in His image***', His breath breathed love and life into the first Adam. Yet in the Garden of Eden, Adam doubted the Word of the Lord, and his action was a rejection of God Himself. At that moment, mankind agreed and aligned with the snake and a spirit of rejection.

I am grateful to Anne Hamilton for pointing out a key to overcoming rejection when she was with us in Bendigo.[52] It is found in the Genesis 4 dialogue between God and Cain ***before*** Abel was killed. Abel's offering was ***accepted*** by the Lord and Cain's offering was ***rejected.*** Cain's anger and disappointment were so deep, it showed in his facial expression. God's word to Cain is for us too.

> *'If you do well, will you not be accepted? And if you do not do well, sin lies at the door. And its desire (sin and rejection) is for you, but you should rule over it.' (Genesis 4:7 NKJV)*

The offerings of Cain and Abel are about worship. That worship can be accepted or rejected by God is a big issue in itself. (But not for us to discuss today!)

Today we will focus on the strategy the Lord gave Cain. It was a word of wisdom as to how to overcome rejection. Cain was not told to 'cast out a demon' of rejection. Cain was told to '*rule over*' rejection. He had to overcome it. God had previously said to Adam—'I have given you dominion'. Now God says to Cain, 'Exercise that dominion'.

We, like Cain, are instructed to rule over rejection, to master it, take dominion over it. As believers we also have access to the victory Jesus had at the cross as He overcame rejection on our behalf.

For me this has been personal. I have needed to overcome incidences of rejection that have at times been overwhelming.

And it has been a recurring pattern. The twins of 'rejection and grumbling' seem to arrive at my heart's door in time to coincide with special and significant events with family or friends. When I have allowed the overwhelming emotions to drown me, I have inevitably let grumbling through the door. Consequently, I have been the one to suffer and miss out on the otherwise joyful occasion!

Sometimes 'rejection' has arrived at my door through the words or actions of others. But sometimes it has been my own interpretations of those words and actions. I have seen this pattern repeated over and over; in my own life and in the lives of many of God's people. Our filters, created by past wounds, warp our perceptions. Whether rejection is real or perceived, it feels awful and crushes our confidence. Yet a choice has to be made. We must choose to overcome.

There are times I have not won the battle. Without exception, each time I failed to overcome, I was the one who missed out on significant opportunities of friendship, fellowship and even special blessings.

Other times I have been victorious. I have really had to press into what Jesus did at the cross. It has sometimes felt like a wrestling match! My flesh has wanted to run away or retaliate. But as I've sought the Lord's help, I have been astonished to watch the Lord supernaturally intervene, reverse circumstances and open up extraordinary blessings.

At the cross, Jesus endured our rejection so we can be accepted. While our heads can rejoice at this wonderful revelation, do our hearts receive it—especially when we feel the sword of rejection through our hearts? Making the most of Jesus' victory is key to our victory. Jesus was 'despised and rejected by men' at the cross. He bore the pain and sorrow we experience because of rejection.

The spirit of rejection has another mate called abandonment. The devil wants to convince us God will not be there for us. It may feel He has already abandoned you. But grab hold of this truth today:

> *'For He Himself has said, 'I will never leave you nor forsake you.' (Hebrews 13:5 NKJV)*

> *The Passion Translation* renders it:
>
> *'I will never leave you alone, never! And I will not loosen my grip on your life!' (Hebrews 13:5 TPT)*

ACTIVATION

Is there a situation of rejection you are facing and need to overcome?

1. Be honest about it before the Lord. Confess it and lift it to Him today.
2. Read, personalise and pray over yourself: Ephesians 1:4-6 Romans 8:15, 28, 29. Remind the spirit realm of the truth of this Word.
3. Praise Him for His breath of life breathing love into you. Give thanks for His strength empowering you to overcome every work of the spirit of rejection.

PRAYER

I thank You, Father, that I am always and dearly loved by You.[53] Thank You for the privilege and honour that You chose me to be Your own. You have created me in Your image. You sent Your only Son to redeem what the devil sought to destroy. It was the greatest act of inclusivity, honour and love! I rejoice that Your dunamis power strengthens me to overcome and Your acceptance is stronger than the enemy's rejection! You have loved me with an everlasting love. I am Your child, Your blood-washed son /daughter. You sent Your only Son to provide the way for me to be accepted and embraced by You. Thank You for the spirit of adoption, of full acceptance of being Your son/daughter. (Romans 8:15) I thank You that I am no longer an unwanted orphan. By the blood of Yeshua, I have been made holy, acceptable and can come near to You. I am so grateful for Your Presence, so I am never alone. And You never abandon or leave me! I am amazed; You sing over me! You have established and written my DNA in a book. Before I was born, You gave me a destiny and a purpose to fulfill—plans that were established in your heart (Ephesians 1:11) I praise You! Amen

---

52. Anne Hamilton spoke on 'Rejection' at Tabernacle of David (Bendigo) March 30th 2019. Anne's message was recorded live and is on Youtube channel of Tabernacle of David (Bendigo)

    https://www.youtube.com/channel/UCSO95qMc35uAJER0sU-qjIg?view_as=subscriber

53. Colossians 3:12 TPT

DAY 17

Father Loves You the Same as Jesus!

'He made us accepted in the Beloved.' (Ephesians 1:6 NKJV)

'His tremendous love that cascades over us would glorify His grace—for the ***same love*** *He has for his Beloved One, Jesus, He has for us.' (Ephesians 1:6 TPT)*

'You live fully in me and now I live fully in them so that they will experience perfect unity, and the world will be convinced that you have sent me, for they will see that You love each one of them with the same passionate love that you have for Me.' (John 17:23 TPT)

Wow! Did you read that amazing statement? 'The ***SAME*** love Father has for His Beloved One, Jesus, He has for us!' Sorry about the capitalisation—but it is worth yelling about! God the Father loves us the same as He loves Yeshua. The Father loves us every bit as much as Yeshua! Can you absorb that? The first time I read that, it almost felt sacrilegious. Then, after getting over the initial shock of the enormity of the statement, I was able to start absorbing and receiving the truth. It is an extraordinary truth. God's love for us is beyond comprehension!

Yet, why is it we struggle to absorb such good news? We easily absorb bad news, right into our innermost being. But what about truth and good news? The statement from Ephesians 1:4-6 is one you need to read and re-read and let it penetrate down deep into those areas of hurt, rejection and doubt. Read it in the various translations. Do that now—go back to the top and re-read the Scripture.

Now read it out aloud, and as well, personalise it. Hear the Father speak these words to you personally. Let the revelation seep deep into your spirit.

'The same love (Father) God has for His Beloved One, Jesus, He has for me!' Now say it again, but this time, put your own name in to replace the generic 'us or me'. *'The same love (Father) God has for His Beloved One, Jesus, He has for (your name)...........................!'*

If you had trouble with yesterday's message about being accepted rather than being rejected, then let this revelation set you free today. Grasping the fact that our heavenly Father has the same love for us as He has for Jesus makes John 3:16 come alive. *'God so loved the world He gave His only Son...'*

I have to say, in recent years I have had a fresh revelation of the Lord as I have started to grasp Ephesians 1 in *The Passion Translation.* Simultaneously, He has dealt with deep roots of rejection and inferiority.

The Holy Spirit has also been doing a deep work across the church to shift our collective thinking and to deliver us from the orphan heart. 'God so loved the world' is not just good theology or a good poster slogan. It is a world changing fact. A fact, if we are honest, many of us struggle to really believe in the depths of our hearts. We know it in our heads, but has it shifted down into the heart?

We have no problems with Father's great love for His Son Yeshua. But the same depth of love for us? We may be able to grasp it about someone else—but me? Yet this is vital if we are to receive His love deep into our soul. Knowing His love in our hearts means we receive His love into those areas of our thoughts and emotions where the devil's lies have lodged. Knowing His love in our heart means His love soaks down into those areas where we have felt unloved, rejected, and not good enough.

Being in His Presence in true worship is the most powerful way to get an accurate and life-changing revelation of the Holy One and His love. Isaiah saw the Lord sitting on His throne. The Lord's robe filled the temple. The sound of heavenly worship caused the door-posts to shake as angels sang; 'Holy, holy, holy'. Isaiah's life was never the same. Let His love transform you heart.[54]

ACTIVATION

1. Spend time in His Presence.
2. Position your heart to receive a fresh revelation of His love.
3. Declare the verse from Ephesians 1 as many times as you need to. *'The same love (Father) God has for His Beloved One, Jesus, He has for me (your name)...........................!'*
4. Thank Him for His amazing love. Start with; 'Thank You, Father, You have the same love for me as You have for Your only begotten Son, Yeshua.'... Now keep thanking Him.
5. Let this powerful, unfathomable love permeate and cascade into every circumstance you are lifting up to Him today.
6. Give thanks for His perfect love removing ***all*** your fears, ***all*** your rejection, and ***all your*** abandonment.

PRAYER

Righteous Father, I have known and believed about the love You have for me. Yet Father, I acknowledge, many times it has only been in my head and hasn't really penetrated into my heart. I ask For Your help today, Holy Spirit. Let Your love be so real. Let it flood into and penetrate every part of my heart. I thank You that Your immeasurable love permeates and soaks into every area of hurt, confusion, doubt and fear. By faith I know You are love. Help me to know Your love in a fresh and tangible way. Father, You are love. You don't try to love like I do. You are love. You created me to be loved. I thank You for Your indescribable love. As I abide in Your love, I abide in You.[55]

Today, as I choose to place my roots deep into Your love, I thank You that I will be filled with all Your fullness. Though Messiah's love is beyond my human understanding, I thank You for it, and receive it into my innermost being.[56]

Messiah loved me and gave His life as a sweet-smelling offering so I can walk in Your love. Thank You for that amazing provision.[57] Holy Spirit, help me to walk in the sweet perfume of Your sacrificial love today. Amen

---

54. Further teaching on this subject is found in the DVD teaching "Transformed by Love" by Ruth Webb

    https://www.tabernacleofdavid.org.au/shop/dvd-teaching-31/transformed-by-love.html

55. 1 John 4:16 NKJV
56. Ephesians 3:17b-19 NKJV
57. Ephesians 5:2 NKJV

DAY 18

Tale of Victim, Grumbling, Self-Pity, & Gratitude

'Even though you planned evil against me, Elohim planned good to come out of it. This was to keep many people alive, as He is doing now.' (Genesis 50:20 GW)

'We know that all things work together for the good of those who love God—those whom he has called according to his plan.' (Romans 8:28 GW)

'He has sent me to provide for all those who grieve in Zion, to give them crowns instead of ashes, the oil of joy instead of tears of grief, and clothes of praise instead of a spirit of weakness.' (Isaiah 61: 3 GW)

Victim was miserable. He had suffered so many losses. The grief was overwhelming. Hope and Faith seemed to have disappeared. And the bodyguards, Goodness and Mercy, had also left. Victim was all alone. Or so he thought.

Just then Grumbling arrived and invited Victim to go to a party hosted by Self-pity. 'Misery loves company, and the cakes are delicious,' Grumbling said to Victim. So, Victim fell for it and went with Grumbling to the party. When they arrived, Victim was encouraged to tell, re-tell, and tell again, every morbid detail of his painful story. Over and over, like a broken record, Victim told the story. With each repetition he grabbed yet another cake. Each time the details were repeated, the cakes seemed to grow in size and richness.

After a while, Victim began to feel heavy in the stomach, even nauseous. Just then, there was a knock at the door. It was Gratitude looking for Victim. 'Father wants you to come home,' Gratitude said to Victim. 'Father said you need to come home before you become too sick to leave.'

By now, Victim was feeling so ill. Even though Gratitude's arrival was jeered by Grumbling and Self-pity, Victim was quietly relieved. Gratitude reassured Victim all the way home. 'Father's house is much safer than Self-pity's parties. The food at those parties are filled with poison and will only make things worse for you. Father is so good. And He has clean clothes waiting for you to change into when we get home.'

'But Father makes me pretend these things didn't happen,' Victim grumbled. 'And they did happen; you can't deny it,' Victim whined and wailed. Gratitude had to exert some tough love. 'No, Father loves you to talk to Him honestly about your situation. But He does need you to change your clothes first and then to find solutions.'

'What's wrong with these clothes?' Victim wailed. Gratitude looked at Victim. 'Look at you,' Gratitude said, 'your clothes are so dirty and so heavy, you can hardly walk in them.' Victim tried to pretend that the clothes were easy to walk in. But it was hard to disguise his dragging feet and lowered head.

Gratitude encouraged Victim. 'Father has the garments of praise waiting for you at home. When we get there, you can take off these heavy garments of depression and hopelessness. When you put on the garments of praise, Father can then help you sort out this mess.'

Gratitude continued to encourage Victim. 'Take strength and courage from Joseph and Jesus. They were both betrayed by those close to them. Though it hurt and it seemed disastrous, they ultimately could not destroy God's plans and purposes. Father used the circumstances like a boomerang to actually destroy the enemies' plans. You have to realise, Father has the best way to deal with these things.'

Gratitude helped Victim take off the heavy, soggy clothes which had been given by Grumbling. While they were changing the clothes, Gratitude said, 'These clothes are too heavy for you to carry. Father's garments of Praise are lightweight and let in the light. When you wear them, you will have hope and joy. Father loves it when you wear these clothes. When you wear the garments of praise, you can tell Father the truth of your story. When you tell Him directly, and without whinging, it's easier for Him to help you.' Gratitude went further; 'And if you let Him, Father will change your name. You will no longer be known as Victim but Victorious.'

ACTIVATION

Are you prone to self-pity? Are you a victim or victorious?

1. Choose to take off the heavy garments of a grumbling victim. Choose to tear up the victim card. Jesus paid the price for you to be victorious.
2. Repent for times of indulging in the cakes at your pity-party!
3. Put on the garment of praise. Keep praising until heaviness lifts and is replaced by hope and joy.
4. Tell Father your story. Bring your requests to Him with thanksgiving. Rejoice for what He is doing—even the things you can't see yet!

PRAYER

Loving and merciful Father, I thank You for Your garments of praise. Being light and joyful, they are so much nicer to wear instead of the heaviness of grumbling which leaves me weak. Though the enemy planned to totally destroy me and Your purposes, I am so grateful You are able to help me outwit the enemy. I thank You—Your plans not only save me, but also include deliverance for many others, as well. I thank You, Father, for Your good and righteous answers and solutions. Amen

DAY 19

Shalom

'Be anxious for nothing, but in everything by prayer and supplication, with thanksgiving, let your requests be made known to God; and the ***peace of God****, which surpasses all understanding, will* ***guard your hearts and minds*** *through Christ Jesus.' (Philippians 4:6,7 NKJV)*

'With perfect peace You will protect those whose minds cannot be changed, because they trust You.'(Isaiah 26:3 GW)

'And His name will be called Wonderful, Counselor, Mighty God, Everlasting Father, Prince of Peace.' (Isaiah 9:6 NKJV)

The Hebrew word for peace is *shalom*. In Israel, shalom is a word of greeting to say 'hello' and 'goodbye'. Some Jewish friends joke that they greet you when you come and when you go because they do not know if they are coming or going!

Seriously, though, shalom is the most beautiful greeting you can ever give. I remember a tricky situation in a relationship. One day the Holy Spirit encouraged me to just greet the person with 'shalom'. Instantly I could sense all apprehension in the other person just melt away. The Prince of Peace removed fear, anxiety, apprehension and strife.

But shalom is much more than the absence of strife. Shalom includes welfare, soundness, wholeness and completeness, with ***nothing missing***! It refers to safety, health, prosperity, and contentment in real estate and relationships.

The 'peace offering' was established in the Tabernacle of Moses, but it was also known as the 'sacrifice of thanksgiving'. Peace and thanksgiving are linked. As mentioned in Day 4, 'Sacrifice of Praise', these two sacrifices were the offerings given to God as acts of worship. Give the Lord thanks and you ***will*** have peace. Thanksgiving and peace are eternally linked in God's kingdom. Try grumbling, and what happens to your peace? It leaves. The correlation between thanks and peace is proven even by science.

Thanksgiving and gratitude do ***not*** deny the trials of life. Some people get religious and pretend that all is well when it is not. Some think thanksgiving means to put on a fake smile and 'praise the Lord' through gritted teeth. It is not about pretentious lips! Gratitude begins in the heart. Jesus taught that what comes out of our mouths actually comes from the heart. (Matthew 15:18) True praise comes out of a grateful heart.

Peace of mind!

Troubling circumstances often rob or disturb our peace—especially in our minds and emotions. But the Lord provides us with a solution. This is how we get peace of mind.

> *'Let your heart be always guided by the peace of the Anointed One, who called you to peace as part of his one body. And always be thankful.' (Colossians 3:15 TPT)*

The footnotes in *The Passion Translation* for the above Scripture says, 'The Greek literally means ***let peace be the umpire of your minds.***'[58]

Troubles usually 'play on our mind'. The mind is a battlefield, but shalom is a protection for our minds. Let shalom be the umpire in the war in our mind! The *New King James Version* says to let God's peace 'rule in your hearts'. God's Word says let God's peace 'control you'. The *Complete Jewish Bible* says to let Messiah's shalom be 'your heart's decision maker'. His peace will impact your emotions, mind and decisions, bringing wholeness and contentment.

Conditional Promise

The condition to experience His shalom is to bring our requests and troubling circumstances to Him ***with gratitude.*** The Scripture says, *'by prayer and supplication, with thanksgiving,* ***let your requests be made known*** *to God'.*[59]

Giving thanks is linked to receiving His peace. Gratitude is not a supplement to shalom, but rather, is an essential component and intrinsically attached to shalom. When we are unwavering in our gratitude toward Him, our minds are flooded with Him. Peace is a bodyguard for the mind!

Many things in life can make us anxious. That is normal. But we can avoid the destructiveness of anxiety by being honest with God. Bring to Him your requests. Do it in prayer—and thanksgiving. Know who God is in the midst of the trials.

Yeshua the Messiah is the Prince of Peace. He ***is*** shalom. We can trust Him to bring us into shalom. When we place our trouble in one hand as an offering to Him, and in the other hand we see who God is, we can give thanks. As we thank Him for who He is, we can find His peace even in the midst of trouble. *Shalom – Peace* is a protection and brings us into wholeness!

ACTIVATION

What circumstances have robbed you of peace and joy? Be intentional and specific.

- Name them and lift them up to Him
- Invite the Prince of peace into your named circumstances today
- Thank Him for penetrating your circumstances with shalom!

PRAYER

Lord, You are Wonderful, Counsellor, Mighty God, Everlasting Father, and the Prince of Peace. You are the substance and provision of my welfare, soundness of mind, wholeness and completeness, with nothing missing.

I thank You, Lord, that every circumstance I have given You today is being made safe, healthy, and prosperous. Prince of Peace, as healer of the breach, You are making my relationships whole and complete in You. I thank You that in regard to these matters I have given You today, Your shalom guards and protects my mind, my emotions and my decisions. Amen

Thank Him—shalom is restoring your joy!

Now make your requests to Him—with thanks.

---

58. *The Passion Translation* footnote (c) for Colossians 3:15

59. Philippians 4:6 NKJV

DAY 20

The Blood of Jesus Is Enough

'He has...wiped out the handwriting of requirements that was against us, which was contrary to us. And He has taken it out of the way, having nailed it to the cross.' (Colossians 2:14-15 NKJV)

'Then I heard a loud voice saying in heaven, 'Now salvation, and strength, and the kingdom of our God, and the power of His Christ have come, for the accuser of our brethren, who accused them before our God day and night, has been cast down. And they overcame him by the blood of the Lamb and by the word of their testimony, and they did not love their lives to the death.' (Revelation 12:10-11 NKJV)

'To Him who loved us and washed us from our sins in His own blood, and has made us kings and priests to His God and Father, to Him be glory and dominion forever and ever. Amen.' (Revelation 1:5, 6 NKJV)

There is power in the blood of Jesus.

My grandmother had a temporary battle with mental illness after she was visited by some religious cult. She had believed their lies and was left devastated. One day she cried out to the Lord for deliverance. She had a supernatural vision of a cup filled with the blood of Jesus. As the Lord ministered to her about the power of the blood of Jesus, her mind was totally restored and healed.

There is power in the blood of Jesus.

Before we were married, Laurence and I were in a Christian Bush band established by our church community. We worked with the evangelism team who would talk to people while we sang the gospel with piano accordion, bush bass, tambourines, whistles and whatever else we could find! We frequently felt resistance as we sang in the Bendigo mall. At those times we would launch into the old Salvation Army hymn 'Power in the Blood'. Without fail, singing about the power of His blood changed the atmosphere. There were times where I could literally sense demons running for their lives!

There is power in the blood of Jesus.

In 2017, a young man walked into our weekly worship watch. He had been released from prison the day before. He had been waiting at the bus stop outside our building but then needed to find a toilet. He was scared to walk into a church, thinking God would zap him because of all his sins. The Holy Spirit zapped him all right—but with love and forgiveness. Over the next few weeks as he came into the church, the blood of Jesus powerfully transformed this former drug dealer and addict.

There is no sin on the planet that the blood of Yeshua cannot cleanse, forgive and atone for. There is no sinner on the planet that the blood of Yeshua cannot change. There is no disturbed mind that the blood of Jesus cannot restore.

In decades past, the phrase 'I plead the blood' was understood and powerfully used. Many supernatural miracles resulted. We have lost the significance of the phrase. It is a legal term. In the heavenly law court, Satan the accuser brings indictments against God's people 24/7. It is true, our sins and crimes against God carry the death penalty. But at the cross, Yeshua took our punishment.

So, consider the court case. The devil is reading out all the charges against us. The judge asks, 'How do you plead? Guilty or not guilty?' We can say, 'I plead the blood of Jesus'.

At the cross, Jesus took our indictment and nailed it to His cross! The penalty has been paid—the devil has no further claims!

There is power in the blood of Jesus.

The blood of Yeshua is enough to silence and shut the mouth of the accuser! The blood of Yeshua is enough to wash clean our record and our hearts. His blood is the most powerful disinfectant to remove every stench and infection caused by sin. The blood of Yeshua speaks. It is a powerful voice in the heavenly courtroom. His blood is a voice that pleads for us mercy and forgiveness. The blood of Yeshua is enough for whatever is tripping you up.

ACTIVATION

- Lift your circumstances to the Lord today.
- Apply and proclaim the powerful blood of Jesus to your situation whether it is physical, emotional or spiritual; sickness, false accusation, finances, or relationships.

PRAYER

Lord, I worship You today. I align with the worship of heaven to honour Yeshua; *'Worthy is the Lamb who was slain To receive power and riches and wisdom, And strength and honor and glory and blessing!'* (Revelation 5:12 NKJV)

Spend time giving thanks for the blood of Yeshua.

I thank You, Lord, that the blood of Yeshua cleanses me from all sin. By Your blood I have been redeemed. Through Your blood I can enter into Your Presence. I give thanks that the blood of Yeshua is enough for my circumstances today. There is no situation Your blood cannot cleanse, heal, or redeem. Amen

Spend time praising and thanking Him for the blood of Yeshua.

DAY 21

Bitter or Better?

'Today I offer you life and prosperity or death and destruction. ***Choose life*** *so that you and your descendants will live.' (Deuteronomy 30:15, 19 GW)*

'See to it that no bitter root springs up and causes trouble, and by it many be defiled.' (Hebrews 12:15 TLV)

Life can throw us some curve balls. When it does; how do we respond? Do we grumble or praise? Our choice affects whether we get bitter or better.

Though I didn't realise it at the time, some 30 years ago my heart was crushed and on the brink of permanent bitterness. The Lord confronted me with a choice: remain bitter or get better. I discovered:

1. When life goes pear-shaped and we experience hurt, loss, or wounding, deep in our heart we either blame God or trust Him.
2. Bitterness will take root to grow a poisonous fruit tree if we do not bring the offence, loss or wound to the Lord.
3. To become bitter or better is a choice.

4. Grumbling feeds a bitter root. Thanksgiving helps to uproot and heal the defiling root.
5. Bitterness is contagious and infects others!

My story began more than 50 years ago. After getting saved at age 11, the Lord called me to music-worship ministry. It began with a commitment to the disciplines of practise and study. Later, while studying music at the Music Conservatorium in Melbourne, the Lord burned into me about King David bringing the Ark into Jerusalem accompanied by prophetic songs. Upon graduation, I taught music in Bendigo (a historic gold town two hours north of Melbourne) and I joined a local Pentecostal church. I quickly found myself on the worship team, and later, I became the music director.

National leaders of that denomination spoke confirming and powerful prophetic words over me about my call in worship, healing, His glory and revival for Australia. Things went well for a while. Then the wheels started to fall off. One day the Apostle of the church told me my 'public ministry was over.' I could not believe what I was hearing. It seemed that, though I had done nothing wrong, the 'vision' of the church had suddenly changed.

Confusion and devastation became a constant fog as I felt a major conflict. In my spirit I knew God's call had *not* been fulfilled. Yet I loved, respected and trusted the church leadership. I could not reconcile the two.

Disappointment and hurt turned to grief, depression and anger. I thought all of God's promises had been smashed! Discouraged and angry, I stopped playing the piano for two years. Sadly, I took my anger out on my young family! The usual challenges of toddlers and pre-schoolers suddenly appeared to be higher than Mount Everest.

One night the Lord showed me my anger and warned me of danger. He gave me a choice. He said I could give Him thanks and get better or remain angry and become bitter and destroyed.

I wrestled with the choice. How could I give thanks when everything I had worked for, dreamt about, and been promised by Him had been taken? And it wasn't my fault! Despite my justifications, I knew the Lord was right—He always is! It was crunch time.

Audience of One

Then the Lord upped the requirement—I was to give thanks at the piano with just Him and me! The choices were getting tougher. But for the sake of my husband and children I needed to get better.

Obedience was both hard and weird. I had never sat at the piano with just Him and me. Previously, I always had a congregation to worship with—but now that was all gone. Every time I went to the piano to worship Him, I wept. Each time my attention turned to the sacrifice of Jesus. As I identified with His suffering, I wept and wept. Each day I went to the piano, healing occurred as He washed away another layer of disappointment and hurt.

Today, from the depths of my heart I am sincerely grateful for that season. Without it, I would not be doing what I am doing today. Thanksgiving was ***the major key*** to recovery. It saved my life, my marriage and family. Through the painful journey I gained revelation about warfare-worship. The Lord taught me how to lead worship, released me into worship ministry and authority to write my first book, *Restoring True Worship*.[60]

How do we praise when our hearts are breaking and aching? It begins with a choice. Focus on Jesus. Consider His suffering for you. Find comfort as you share in His suffering. Each day, find one thing you can be thankful for. Then look for more things you can truly give thanks for. Start small.

Our circumstances may or may not change. But our heart posture will. A changed attitude brings recovery. Even if circumstances remain, gratitude causes us to see differently and gain a new perspective. If we only think about negative and harmful circumstances, we can actually cause brain damage.

At first, I thought my circumstances were a disaster. Today I rejoice. It was the best thing that ever happened to me. Like Joseph, the journey filled with tests enabled the original vision and call to be fulfilled!

One letter Difference between bitter and better: i or e?

When life is tough and we focus on 'i', we get entrapped with self-pity and bitterness. It can lead to dis-ease. It infects others. It causes us to miss our call and destiny. The bitter route spirals down to frustration and grief.

When we die to self and focus on Elohim, we shift from the 'i' of bitter to the 'e' of better. Bitterness gives way to getting better as we invite Him into our situation. Elohim is the Hebrew word for 'supreme God'. When He is above every other 'god', we are on the path to recovery! Bitterness can turn loss into a 'god' as we place self-interest above His.

Gratitude and thanksgiving are the difference between bitter and better. Gratitude is the path to Elohim, His healing, restoration and intervention. The speed of recovery varies, depending on personality, severity of loss, and support available. Don't be tripped up if healing is slow—He knows the best road to recovery. Whether fast or slow, healing is healing.

ACTIVATION

1. Honestly write your bitter circumstances on a piece of paper, and then lift it to the Lord. Acknowledge your need of His help. Admit where these circumstances have robbed you of His peace and joy. (Name them before Him..............)
2. Pray in the Spirit.
3. Make a choice to get better.
4. Ask Holy Spirit for a strategy that works for you.
5. Make your request to Him with thanksgiving.

PRAYER

I thank You, Holy Spirit, You are my comforter, my helper to assist me through life.

Holy Spirit help me to choose life today. Strengthen me to choose praise in the midst to these challenges. I thank you, Holy Spirit. You are my helper—help me say yes to gratitude, yes to becoming better and yes to letting go of bitterness.

I thank You that the blood of Jesus is cleansing my soul so my decisions are cleansed to make right choices. I thank you, Holy Spirit, that Your grace is sufficient for me today. Your strength is made perfect in my weakness. Thank You for helping me to choose life. Amen

60. https://www.tabernacleofdavid.org.au/shop/book-32/restoring-true-worship.html

DAY 22

Nothing Can Separate from His Love

'Who shall separate us from the love of Christ? Shall tribulation, or distress, or persecution, or famine, or nakedness, or peril, or sword? ...For I am persuaded that neither death nor life, nor angels nor principalities nor powers, nor things present nor things to come, nor height nor depth, nor any other created thing, shall be able to separate us from the love of God which is in Christ Jesus our Lord.' (Romans 8:35, 38-39 NKJV)

Nothing—not even the most challenging of circumstances, can separate you from God's love. No, not even the ones you are walking through right now. Nothing, absolutely ***nothing*** can separate you from the love of God.

There are times that it may feel like His love is a million miles away. But even when life is tough, the truth is, we ***cannot*** be separated from His love!

Prior to the verses above, Paul said we cannot explore the depths of God's love—it is too high, wide, and deep. The old spiritual song says: 'So high we can't get over it, so low we can't get under it, so wide we can't get around it...oh rock a my soul'. Assurance of His love can soothe the most troubled soul.

As Hitler's troops were sweeping through Amsterdam, the Ten Boom family were hiding Jews in their home at the back of their watchmaker shop. Due to betrayal, the family was found out and imprisoned. While in the despair of Ravensbrück concentration camp (near Berlin), Corrie Ten Boom said, 'There is no pit so deep, that God's love is not deeper still.'

It is hard to imagine a pit deeper than the Holocaust and being in one of the concentration camps! Yet as Corrie trusted the Lord, she found strength. Did this trust activate the miracle of her release? Only God knows. Having visited Sachsenhausen concentration camp and Wannasee, where the Holocaust had been 'devised'; I can only conclude that Corrie had an extraordinary, supernaturally overwhelming, revelation and encounter with Father's amazing love.

Corrie realised that even Ravensbrück concentration camp could not separate her from God's love. Paul also faced massive persecution when he wrote, '*There is nothing in the universe with the power to separate us from God's love*'! (Romans 8:38 TPT)

Consider the worst scenario of life. Maybe it's one you are walking through at the moment. Whatever it is, it ***cannot*** separate you from God's love.

Ask for a fresh revelation of His love—it's a love that cannot be measured! It's a love that is deeper than the worst challenge.

ACTIVATION

- Spend time praising the Lord for His unfailing love.
- Ask Him for a fresh revelation of His love…and thank Him for His love penetrating your heart.
- Lift up your personal circumstances today and thank Him that this situation cannot separate you from His great and wonderful love!

PRAYER

Righteous Father, You are my King and you reign over all gods! Your tender love for me continues forever! I rejoice. You are above, and reign over, every person of high rank or noble office! I praise You for Your powerful miracles. There is no-one like You. You are the only miracle working God! And Your tender love for me is forever! (Psalm 136:1-4)

Your love never fails.

Your love drives fear far from my heart. I am so grateful that there is ***nothing*** that can separate me from Your love. 'Troubles, pressures and problems are unable to come between me and heaven's love….There is nothing in the universe with the power to separate me from God's love. There is nothing in my present or future circumstances that can weaken His love.'[61]

Your tender love for me is forever! Amen

Continue praising Him for His great and inexhaustible love.

61. Based on Romans 8:35, 38 TPT

DAY 23

His Word Is Forever

'Forever, O Lord, Your word is settled in heaven.' (Psalm 119:89 NKJV)

'Your faithfulness flows from one generation to the next; all that You created sits firmly in place to testify of You. By Your decree everything stands at attention, for all that You have made serves You...I've learned that there is nothing perfect in this imperfect world except your words...Truth's shining light guides me in my choices and decisions; the revelation of your word makes my pathway clear... Truly, your message of truth means more to me than a vault filled with the purest gold. Every word you speak, every truth revealed, is always right and beautiful to me, for I hate what is phony or false. Your marvelous words are living miracles.' (Psalm 119:90-91, 96, 105, 127-129 TPT)

There are three wonderful reassuring concepts in the Scriptures above. First is the strength and reliability of God's Word; second is His faithfulness; and third is eternity. These three provide us with great comfort, assurance, security and a solid anchor.

In life, anxiety and apprehension come through fear, insecurity and doubt. We especially are afraid of failure – things going askew or ending – bringing us disappointments, and feelings of betrayal and trust broken. So much damage is caused by broken promises. Our words are often conditional or limited. Unfortunately, forever promises are rare in our society as we have sadly become too accustomed to broken covenants. Worse, we rarely understand what covenant really is, even within the Church.

Even though it can be hard to grasp, yet God ***is*** faithful to His Word. When we have been disappointed, we can find trusting God's Word tricky. And the devil does everything to undermine our trust in the credibility and reliability of God's Word.

But God's Word is trustworthy. God is faithful to His Word. And His Word is attached to eternity! He is the forever God. He is the beginning and the end. His Word is established, settled and placed in heaven forever.

God's Word is truth. Jesus is the living Word; He is the way, truth and life. God is who He says He is. The words He speaks are steadfast and immovable. It is like they are set in concrete. He does not change. What He says does not change. His promises are reliable. They are trustworthy. His Word is attached to the faithfulness of His holy name.

His words are settled permanently. His Word is not for one day, one week, one year or even one lifetime—but they are from one generation to another. They are forever. There is no end date or 'use by' date.

A time when His Word will vanish does ***not*** exist! Though eternity is a difficult concept for our finite minds to grasp, yet time without end is the basis of our belief of salvation and heaven when we die. If His words about eternal life are true—so too are all His other words.

Whatever your circumstances today—His words will supersede every trial, every disease, every temptation, every injustice, every betrayal, and every disappointment.

In response to His Word and His decrees, the heavens and earth were created. (Psalm 148:5,6 Hebrews 11:3) So too, His Word and decrees will sustain and strengthen us today. By His Word, we have hope for tomorrow. We may not know what will happen tomorrow, but we do know who holds the future!

ACTIVATION

1. Today, open your mouth as you read aloud the Scriptures at the top. As you read, ***inhale*** the Word of God! Absorb it into your innermost being. Let it touch your circumstances today. Let His Word renew your hope and joy. (Psalm 119:131 TPT)
2. Option: repeat #1 using the following Scriptures: Isaiah 40:8; 1 Peter 1:25; Matthew 24:35; Psalm 148:5,6; Hebrews 11:3.
3. Allow His forever promises to soak into your circumstances today.

PRAYER

Righteous, loving and faithful Father, You are faithful to Your Word, and to Your covenants. I rejoice in Your faithfulness today. I rejoice in Your Word. I thank You that I can rely on Your Word.

I bless You Lord; it was by Your Word You Created the heavens and earth. I thank You, Lord; Your Word sustains life on earth, and it sustains my life today. I bless You, Lord; Your Word is settled in heaven forever, Your Word is trustworthy and dependable for all time.

I rejoice that Your Word does not return void and has answers for me today. As I lift my circumstances before You today, (name these before Him_______________), I place Your Word above every situation. I proclaim Your Word is above my situation. Your Word supersedes my situation. Your Word is settled in heaven forever. My trials are temporary, but Your Word is forever. Hallelujah. Amen

Continue praising Him.

His eternal and trustworthy Word is
penetrating your circumstances.

DAY 24

Truth Sets Free

'The truth will set you free.' (John 8:32 GW)

'Jesus said to him, 'I am the way, the truth, and the life.' (John 14:6 NKJV)

'Use the truth to make them holy. Your words are truth!' (John 17:17 GW)

Jesus, or Yeshua in Hebrew, is the living Word. He is truth. Truth sets us free. His truth liberates us, guides us, and cleans us up—making us holy as He is holy! The Old Testament calls the Word *Torah*, or teaching. Jesus did not come to abolish the Torah, but to fulfil it—after all, He ***is*** the Word![62]

In our current world, truth is vital to protect us. Proverbs 6:23-24 says that the Torah, the Word, the commands of God, are a powerful light to instruct us and to protect us from seduction and immorality.

One of the biggest struggles for Christians amidst the pressures of culture wars and political correctness is how to remain faithful to God's truth, yet simultaneously love those who violate those truths. Hating the sin and simultaneously loving the sinner is not easy. It's even harder in the current environment of activist groups railing and litigating against Christians for standing on the Word.

Aeroplanes need two wings to fly. Only an exceptional pilot and aircraft could survive with one! On May 1, 1983, an Israeli pilot of an F-15 was involved in a training mishap and had a mid-air collision with a Skyhawk. Unbeknown to the pilot of the F-15, one wing had been sheared off. Miraculously, he landed safely! But ordinarily, a plane needs two wings!

Jesus is both truth and love. They are like the two wings of an aircraft to keep it balanced and able to fly. Truth without love can be brutal and legalistic. Love without truth will lead to gushy, sentimental compromise.

Jesus not only manifested truth and love—these characteristics are His nature. He is truth. He is love. When we align with the Word and nature of Jesus, we will have a better balance.

Cars whose wheels have good alignment are more efficient and easier to drive. Cars are a metaphor for our lives and ministries. When we accept and receive both His truth and love deep into our soul, our lives are aligned with God's plumb line. The plumb line of God comes from His truth and love, and will transform us. When we align with the One who is truth, love and holiness, life goes much better and is more efficient!

This next Scripture is like getting a good wheel alignment. This is what occurs when we align with the Word of truth—Yeshua!

> *'He sent His word and healed them, And delivered them from their destructions. Oh, that men would give thanks to the Lord for His goodness, And for His wonderful works to the children of men! Let them sacrifice the sacrifices*

of thanksgiving, And declare His works with rejoicing.' (Psalm 107: 20-22 NKJV)

His Word, His truth, Yeshua, is sent to heal and deliver. This passage was first written about Israel in the wilderness. It is also true of Yeshua coming to earth. And it is also true today for whatever situation is threatening or troubling you.

Yeshua, the Word, the truth—comes to heal and deliver from every destruction! The Hebrew word for destruction means to fall in a pit, even a grave. His Word, His truth, Yeshua, the one who saves; is sent to deliver us from disaster and every pit we fall into. The root of the word for destruction is *shachah*, which is about bowing down in worship—either to God or an idol. Idolatry will land us in a pit of destruction. Turning to the Lord and bowing to Him in true worship will bring us into all truth and He will heal and deliver.

No wonder we are exhorted to 'give thanks to the Lord for His goodness'. Like the Psalmist, alignment with the truth will deliver us from destruction. Such deliverance is good reason to give thanks and to rejoice.

ACTIVATION

1. Give thanks to the Lord for His truth, His Word, His love, Yeshua…
2. Speak to the Lord honestly about your circumstances, and especially any tension between truth and love. Lift your circumstances to Him.

PRAYER

Righteous Father, I come to Your throne of grace today. I thank You for Jesus the living Word. Your Word is healing me from the effect of every trip and fall. Your Word is delivering me from every destruction. You are rescuing me from pits of despair. I thank you for Your freedom and all Your good works. I praise You. I rejoice in You today. Your truth is setting me free today. Amen

Sing or use the words of the old song over your situation;

'It's setting me free, this Holy Ghost power,
It's setting me free, this very hour.'[63]

Rejoice.

62. Matthew 5:17

63. "It's Setting Me Free, this Holy Ghost power". Written in the 1950s by Roy Turner, all his songs were birthed in a time of revival. The Glory People Fellowships were based in England. Often his songs were created spontaneously in meetings. www.glorypeople.org

DAY 25

Joy Is Strength in Times of Loss

'The Spirit of the Lord God is upon me...to give them beauty for ashes, The oil of joy for mourning, The garment of praise for the spirit of heaviness; That they may be called trees of righteousness...' (Isaiah 61:1–3 NKJV)

'Therefore with joy you will draw water From the wells of salvation.' (Isaiah 12:3 NKJV)

'Do not sorrow, for the joy of the Lord is your strength.' (Nehemiah 8:10 NKJV)

'And now my head shall be lifted up above my enemies all around me; Therefore I will offer sacrifices of joy in His tabernacle; I will sing, yes, I will sing praises to the Lord.' (Psalm 27:6 NKJV)

'In Your presence is fullness of joy; At Your right hand are pleasures forevermore.' (Psalm 16:11 NKJV)

Joy is not only a fruit of the Spirit, joy is also a specific anointing to strengthen us in times of loss and mourning.

Loss is something we all experience at some time; it is a part of life. Loss of health, a loved one, relationships, job, finances—and often linked with hopes and dreams. Loss is painful. Grief and sorrow are natural consequences.

Yet we can mourn in a godly or ungodly way. Godly mourning is to continue trusting God—even with thanksgiving. Even when loss is confusing, we can trust God. (As per this 40 days of gratitude.) Even in the valley of the shadow of death, we are assured of His protection from evil because He is with us. It may be a foggy valley, but we can trust He is there and will bring us safely through. The Spirit of God releases His anointing oil to give us joy even in the midst of mourning. Joy is a special anointing filled with balm, shalom and healing.

Yet the enemy seeks to exploit us in times of loss. The devil tempts us to mourn in ungodly ways, to focus on the loss instead of the Giver of life. The devil tempts us to grumble, complain and wallow in self-pity, and then subjects us to demonic torment and further trauma.

Without the Lord's oil of joy to sustain us and help us through, demonic spirits will impose unhealthy mourning and grief to weakens us, thus increasing ageing and illness! (Psalm 31:9 TPT) That is why Nehemiah encouraged the Jews. He assured them the key to avoiding sorrow was, '*The joy of the Lord is your strength.*' (Nehemiah 8:10 NKJV)

Joy comes as we gaze upon Yeshua and are united with Him. Joy lifts shame from our countenance and removes mourning.[64]

Consider the simple profound song:

> 'Turn your eyes upon Jesus,
> Look full in His wonderful face,
> And the things of earth will grow strangely dim
> In the light of His glory and grace.'[65]

Joy is not dependent on 'happy' circumstances. Happiness is dependent on happenings. Joy comes from the Spirit of God who is not influenced by our happenings. Joy is like an internal spring that bubbles up regardless of events on earth. The eternal spring of joy comes from the Spirit of God. He is joy.

Gratitude, praise and joy are indelibly linked. Gratitude and praise are His language. When gratitude comes from our heart—joy ***will*** bubble up.

ACTIVATION

1. Choose to gaze upon Yeshua today.
2. Choose joy to be your strength today!
3. Go back to the Scriptures for today; meditate on them, personalise them, and use them as a prayer of thanks.

PRAYER

Righteous heavenly Father, Papa, You are the giver of joy.

I thank you for the eternal fountain of joy which comes from Your Spirit. I thank You that Your joy comes as a fresh anointing for me today. I thank You for this anointing to strengthen my soul. I am so grateful it is a balm and healing for my losses. As I gaze on You, my loss comes into perspective. I align my heart with Your throne. I surrender all confusion and thank you for Your joy to help me through. Amen

If loss is weakening you now or has weakened you in the past:

- Lift the situation to Him and thank Him for His joy to heal and strengthen your soul (thoughts, emotions, choices).
- Repent for the times you allowed the enemy to exploit your loss.
- Now praise Him. He is Lord of time and space. There is no loss (past or present) that is beyond His power or creativity. Give Him thanks for the way His creative power is penetrating your circumstances.

Continue to speak to Him from your heart.

---

64. Psalm 34:5 TPT

65. Written by Helen H. Lemmel, 1922 © 1922. Public Domain

DAY 26

Thanksgiving Is His Will

'Rejoice always, pray without ceasing, in everything give thanks; for this is the will of God in Christ Jesus for you.' (1 Thessalonians 5:16-18 NKJV)

Probably among the top ten prayers of every Christian would be; 'Lord, what do You want me to do? What is Your will for my life?' The prayer reflects the deeper issues of identity and destiny. Our questions are usually seeking answers for major life decisions of career, where to live and marriage.

He has already told us some things He wants us to do. He wants us to be grateful for each part of our journey as it unfolds. What if each step, including failures, is important to find our final destiny? If giving thanks is His will, then it must be important.

Imagine if we were able to eavesdrop on each other's private conversations with the Lord. I wonder how accurate this dialogue might be?

Human: Lord, what do You want me to do today?

Jesus: In everything give thanks.

Human: Are you kidding me? That's it?

Jesus: (Silence)

Human: How will that help resolve all these big problems I'm facing today?

Jesus: Trust Me; I've got it.

Human: But, Lord something needs to be *done*! It can't go on; 'xyz' needs to be fixed!

Jesus: Silence

Me: But I need to know what is going on—now! Why is this happening?

Jesus: (Silence)

Human: Whinge, moan grumble…

Jesus: Silence.

Jesus: In everything give thanks, for this is the will of God.

Our humanity is at odds with the wisdom of God. His thoughts and ways are so far above ours.

When I was single, I prayed and prayed about finding a godly husband. It was such a frequent prayer, it became a focus—and I got very frustrated. But one day, probably in response to His challenge, I began to thank God for His answer. Very soon the pressure lifted, and I started to enjoy life. Some months later, when I met my dearly beloved, I had nearly forgotten about the request! Giving thanks removed my focus from the need to the Problem Solver.

Abraham was told to leave his family and country. He didn't know where he was going—but the Lord did. His obedience led to the creation of the nation of Israel and the Promised Land for that nation.

DAY 26

Some thirty years ago I faced situations where I identified with Abraham. We were called 'out' of what we had known but had no idea 'where' we were going—or how we would get there. I had no idea where His instructions would lead. Today I can look back at an amazing journey. Some steps were small, some steps seemed impossible. But each step was vital. Each step required obedience. And very often my only instruction was to—give thanks! Each step of obedience formed the path He wanted me to walk on! Each small step of obedience led to the next step unfolding.

When circumstances are difficult, or plain bad, and especially when they are caused by evil, it is not always easy to give thanks for 'everything'. Some would suggest that there are certain things we should not give thanks for. But giving thanks 'in everything' is different to 'for everything.'

We can honestly tell the Lord our struggles and pain, but in it, also acknowledge that God never changes, He is still good. Giving thanks is trusting Him to give you the grace needed to get through. Giving thanks is knowing He can turn our mourning into dancing. Giving thanks is an act of obedience.

Gratitude and praise are the language, environment and power of heaven. Gratitude and thanks invite the Lord into our situation. Gratitude to God amidst life's troubles is not denial, but an act of obedience and faith. It is praise at these times that stirs heaven and defeats hell. I have experienced angelic visitations in worship services when I have by faith given thanks even though my heart feels crushed.

PRAYER

Father, Yeshua travailed in the Garden of Gethsemane. With blood pouring out of His pores, He surrendered His will; 'Father, Your will, not mine.'

I thank You that in Gethsemane the blood of Yeshua redeemed my will. Today I apply the blood of Yeshua to my will. Today I choose to give You thanks. Today I choose to praise You regardless of my circumstances.

I lift my circumstances to You: (name them)

____

Over each of these situations, I declare You are good. I praise You, I exalt Your holy name. You are worthy of all praise. Amen

Continue to praise Him. By faith, give Him thanks.

Thank Him for what He is doing that you cannot see yet!

DAY 27

He Bore All Our Grief and Sorrows

'Surely He has borne our griefs And carried our sorrows; Yet we esteemed Him stricken, Smitten by God, and afflicted. But He was wounded for our transgressions, He was bruised for our iniquities; The chastisement for our peace was upon Him, And by His stripes we are healed.' (Isaiah 53:4,5 NKJV)

'He himself carried our sins in his body on the cross so that we would be dead to sin and live for righteousness. Our instant healing flowed from his wounding.' (1 Peter 2: 24 TPT)

Some suggest that the 39 stripes laid on Yeshua's back were for each of the 39 categories of diseases apparently known to man.[66] Under Jewish law, prisoners could be given forty lashes, but usually only received thirty-nine because many died after receiving forty. Receiving one short of death, the stripes of Jesus were for our sin, sickness and pain—physical and emotional.

In the year 2007 I was bedridden for a month with whooping cough. In the midst of the illness, I was trying to organise a major conference plus deal with a severe betrayal in our ministry. A friend came to visit and pray. As she prayed, I lay there with tears rolling down my cheeks with no strength to keep going. I was sure I was all done. Finished!

Some days later I heard in my spirit the Lord (and perhaps angels?) singing the old hymn, 'What a friend we have in Jesus, all our sins and griefs to bear.' A little spark of hope flickered. Another friend sent an article about how the special friends of Jesus are those who are poor and outcast.

I began to remember and take hold of Isaiah 53. I remembered Derek Prince's teaching and encouragement to take Scripture like medicine—3 times a day! So, each day I took a dose of Isaiah 53. I literally spoke it and took it into my innermost being.

After some time, I started to write a song, 'By His Stripes'. As I would take another dose of Isaiah 53, I would get one bar of music. Another dose of Isaiah 53, and another bar of music. It took a month to write the song! Considering soon after this I wrote another song in one hour, 'By His Stripes' was one of the slowest songs I have *ever* written. However, it was definitely impacting. By the time the song was completed, I was out of bed.

Since recording the song on our album 'Holy One', there have been ***many*** testimonies of healing as people listened to this song. One friend had a cancer on her leg. Each day she played the song and took a dose of Isaiah 53. Her leg was healed.

Do you need healing today? If you have the CD— play the song today.[67] If not, read the words. Pray them. By faith absorb them into your innermost being!

'By His stripes we are healed
And by His wounds we're made whole
By His stripes we are healed
And by His wounds we're made whole
Ev'ry pain and ev'ry grief
Y'shuah bore them on the cross
Iniquities were laid on Him
And by his blood we're reconciled
And by His stripes we are healed.
Broken bodies, broken hearts
Broken promises and broken dreams
The man of sorrows is known to grief
He has suffered more than any man
Jesus, Jesus, Jesus, Jesus
Friend of the father-less
Friend of the poor, Friend of those forsaken,
He's a friend of the broken
Man of sorrows took the pain
Nailed it to His cross and gave life in exchange
For He has triumphed gloriously
Love extinguished flames of hate
Life and hope by the power of His cross. [68]

© 2007 Ruth Webb

He bore every grief, sorrow, betrayal, rejection, loneliness, and loss. He is a special friend to those who are at their lowest. He bore every disease, physical wound and pain. He bore sin and iniquity and all their consequences. He bore generational sins and curses. He bore betrayal, division and strife so we can have shalom.

We are to bring Him our pain and suffering and exchange it for His health, wholeness, and blessing. The best way to make the exchange is to thank Him for what He has done. And as we do this, it is no longer our pain, our injury, our wound—when we make the exchange, they now are His! And we get His blessings—health, and wholeness.

ACTIVATION

1. Lift to Him the circumstance causing you pain and sorrow.
2. Decree today's Scriptures over your situation.
3. Personalise the same Scriptures to thank Him for bearing your suffering.

PRAYER

Thank You, Yeshua, for bearing every pain, sorrow, disease, strife, curse, sin. Bless His holy name.

Thank You for healing me and giving me wholeness, peace, forgiveness, and joy. Amen

By faith and with praise, receive His blessing of healing, wholeness, and peace.

---

66. "The 7 Places Jesus Shed His Blood" by Larry Huch (Whitaker House 2000)
67. Available as a digital download www.tabernacleofdavid.org.au
68. Album "Holy One". Track 3 "By His Stripes" 2009 Ruth Webb, Tabernacle of David (Bendigo) Digital download https://www.tabernacleofdavid.org.au/shop/cd-29/holy-one-digital.html

DAY 28

Under His Wings

Take a moment to read all of Psalm 91—here are a few excerpts.

> *'He who dwells in the secret place of the Most High Shall abide under the shadow of the Almighty. I will say of the Lord, 'He is my refuge and my fortress; My God, in Him I will trust.' Surely He shall deliver you from the snare of the fowler And from the perilous pestilence. He shall cover you with His feathers, And under His wings you shall take refuge; His truth shall be your shield and buckler. You shall not be afraid of the terror by night, Nor of the arrow that flies by day, Nor of the pestilence that walks in darkness, Nor of the destruction that lays waste at noonday.' (Psalm 91:1-6 NKJV)*

Every Passover, the Jewish people remember their extraordinary deliverance from the tyrant Pharaoh. When Israel met with the Lord at Mount Sinai, He said to them, "You have seen what I did to the Egyptians, and how I carried you on eagles' wings'. (Exodus 19:4 NKJV)

On our lounge-room wall we have a painting by Anna Mendez called 'Deliverance from Egypt'. It is an amazing picture of a very large eagle dominating the symbols of Egypt. Symbolic of the divine eagle, the eagle in the picture is so large it does not fit in the frame. Only the eagle face, one wing and the start of the other wing is seen. Coming from the eagle is a powerful light beam. Underneath the large eagle, and only one eighth of the whole picture—you see Israel coming out of Egypt! On the bottom right hand side of the picture is a pyramid and Syrinx. On the left hand of the bottom section is Israel walking through the parted Red Sea.

The divine eagle:

- is huge compared to the tyranny of Egypt.
- carried and protected Israel—and will do the same for you.

What big obstacle do you need protection from today? Do you need deliverance from some tyranny, a spirit of Pharaoh, a spirit of anti-Christ? Are any of these making life difficult in your nation, workplace, family or church?

When things go wrong, bad news arrives, disappointments come, or we feel ashamed—where do we go? As a child, I used to run into a wardrobe as a hiding place. Instead of running to false comforters and refuges[69], the safest place for us to run and hide is under the shadow of the Almighty! His wings are a safe resting place. He ***will*** protect us ***when*** we run to Him. Not only does he protect us, He will also carry us through!

ACTIVATION

1. Meditate on the size and protection of the Lord today.
2. Lift your circumstances to Him. Lay Psalm 91 over your situation.
3. Our prayer today is based on a few verses of Psalm 91. Continue to personalise and thank Him from the whole Psalm. If there are any sections your heart cannot say with confidence, then stop and ask His help. Then thank the Lord for strengthening your faith and for His supernatural assurance, calm and help, even when things are overwhelming and scary.

PRAYER

'Lord God, You are such a safe and powerful place for me to find refuge! You are a proven help in time of trouble—more than enough and always available whenever I need You. Thank You for Your peace and assurance to take my fear even when every structure of support crumbles away. I thank You that I can trust You and not be afraid even when the earth quakes and shakes, moving mountains and casting them into the sea. For the raging roar of stormy winds and crashing wave cannot erode my faith in You.' (Based on Psalm 46:1-3 TPT) Amen

Spend some time praising Him. He is so much bigger than your circumstances, and He is a your shield and comfort.

69. Recommended reading: Anne Hamilton. *Hidden in the Cleft: True and False Refuges. Strategies of the Threshold, #4.* QLD, Australia: Armour Books, 2019.

DAY 29

Every Blessing When God Is for Me

'Every spiritual blessing in the heavenly realm has already been lavished upon us as a love gift from our wonderful heavenly Father, the Father of our Lord Jesus—all because he sees us wrapped into Christ. This is why we celebrate him with all our hearts!' (Ephesians 1:3 TPT)

Have you ever said or inferred: 'If only I had__________ (fill in the blank), then I would be happy?'

Would such a sentiment be a grumble or a praise? To help you decide the answer, consider the definition of the two words. The word 'grumble' means to be discontent. And the word 'gratitude' means to express appreciation.

Now re-think the first sentence in the context of its definitions. Is the phrase, 'If I only had__________' an expression of discontent or appreciation?

Proverbs 30 lists four things that are insatiable and never satisfied. The grave, the womb, thirsty soil, and fire. (Proverbs 30:15-16) Wanting more can be dissatisfaction with what we currently have. Of course, it can also be a need we have. For example, without water we die. Though wanting water is a need, according to Exodus 15:24, Israel was caught complaining about the lack of water. The human default to grumbling also revealed fear, doubt and dissatisfaction with Moses and God.

Faith, gratitude and satisfaction go together. Our sufficiency is found in Him. Our loving heavenly Father has given us every blessing that heaven has to give us! According to Ephesians 1:3, we have already received ***every*** blessing. These are not a ***few blessings*** or even ***some blessings.*** It is ***every*** blessing we need! God cannot give us any more because He has already given everything!

- He has given us His Son to be our Messiah. His blood purifies and reconciles us to God. He is the first fruit of the dead, enabling us to embrace a new nature—resurrection life!
- He has given the Holy Spirit to comfort, help and guide us. He is a fire to sanctify, make holy, and perfect our praise.
- His Word sustains and nourishes us like bread.
- He supplies all our need from out of the abundant riches of His glory![70]

'If God is for us, who can be against us?' (Romans 8:36 NKJV)

'Who then would dare to accuse those whom God has chosen in love to be His? God himself is the judge who has issued his final verdict over them—"Not guilty!"'... 'Who then is left to condemn us? Certainly not Jesus, the Anointed One! For He gave his life for us, and even more than that, He has conquered death and is now risen,

exalted, and enthroned by God at His right hand. So how could He possibly condemn us since He is continually praying for our triumph?' (Romans 8:31, 33, 34 TPT)

God's fingerprints are all over your life. Can you see them? Sure, the devil has tried to obliterate God's fingerprints—and you in the process! But like contours on the land, His fingerprints are on your history, your DNA, on your circumstances, and on your potential. God's love is greater than the devil's hatred!

Have you ever felt caught between God's love and the devil's hate? Who wins the tug-o-war, is in your hands. It largely depends on whether you grumble or give thanks! God's love prevails when we praise and express appreciation for the things we already have. The devil's hate prevails when we grumble and moan about things we feel are missing. It is a choice.

Is someone or something against you today? Is there an accusation or condemnation? Do you feel you need more favour or kindness?

When God acquits us with 'not guilty', then every other opinion is invalid and irrelevant. God is the righteous judge, and He has the last word. When God is for us—not one person can successfully be against us!

When a powerful King is on your side—who would dare to challenge you? If a President of a nation issues a pardon—who can undo his decree? When a supreme court acquits a person of false charges—who can challenge the verdict? If heaven's army is behind you—who would dare take you on? If God has given you everything you need—why would you whinge about things you feel are missing?

ACTIVATION

1. Name ten blessings in your life. Include a few clear signs of the Lord's fingerprints on your life.

2. Slowly and loudly, read through Romans 8: 31-39.

3. Thank Him for His blessings and help. Rejoice. When the righteous judge forgives and pardons you; no government, no demon can successfully be against you.

4. Lift any challenging circumstances to Him. As you bring your 'stuff' to Him, take communion. Repent if you have been grumbling and agreeing with the devil. Focus on the blood; pray the blood Scriptures over your mind, emotions and decisions. Sing songs about the blood. Thank Him there is no one left to condemn you.

5. Now pray over all your circumstances.

PRAYER

Righteous Father, I am so blessed. I am so grateful Your fingerprints are all over my life. Thank You for every good gift I have already received from You. You have given to me every blessing from heaven—You have not withheld anything I need to get through today.

Thank You for Your endless love. You are for me today! The Creator of heaven and earth is for me. I am so grateful Your thoughts are toward me and You want the best for me.

I am so grateful You have given me all that I need to overcome and to be victorious. Thank You for Your best gift when You gave Your only Son, whose life and blood enable me to live. You have given me Your Spirit to guide me, help me and comfort me through life's trials. Your Spirit helps me to make wise decisions and to walk circumspectly through life. Your Word sustains me like food. Thank You, Father, that You provide for my every need from out of Your glory realms through Your Son Yeshua. Amen

70. Philippians 4:19

DAY 30

Greater Is He within Me

'You are of God, little children, and have overcome them [spirits of antichrist], because He who is ***in you*** *is* ***greater*** *than* ***he*** *who is* ***in*** *the* ***world****.' (1 John 4:4 NKJV)*

'Then David said to the Philistine, "You come to me with a sword, with a spear, and with a javelin. But ***I come to you in the name of the Lord of hosts****, the God of the armies of Israel, whom you have defied. This day the Lord will deliver you into my hand, and I will strike you and take your head from you... that all the earth may know that there is a God in Israel."' (1 Samuel 17:45–46 NKJV)*

The David - Goliath metaphor is frequently used, even by secular people, to illustrate small ordinary people facing giant circumstances or corporations. However, Biblical giants are not just metaphors. The likes of Goliath were physically and spiritually huge! Even more sinister is the fact giants were considered to be the offspring of women procreating with Nephilim, i.e. fallen angels, or demons.[71]

Demonic powers hate God. It was these giants Israel had to overcome to enter into their inheritance.[72]

Spirits of antichrists, (anti-Messiah) as suggested in 1 John 4 are akin to demonic giants. They hate God with a passion and target anything or anyone with God's fingerprints on them. They also seek to replace God with a counterfeit.

Many antichrist spirits are active today in media, government, education, and arts. It is possible you are facing a giant pressuring you to compromise at work, your career, your family, community, and even in your church. The abortion industry has a giant behind it to destroy a generation—just like Pharaoh and Herod did before the deliverer arrived! The LGBT agenda has a spiritual giant behind it seeking to pressure and intimidate families and children concerning gender fluidity.

When David, the young worshipper, saw Goliath—he saw the situation in the spirit realm. He was not afraid. He had a revelation of the 'Lord of Hosts'. As we contend for nations, we need a fresh revelation of the Lord of Hosts.

In Hebrew, Lord of Hosts is 'Yahweh Tsebaoth' and refers to a massive army. We often think of heavenly hosts as only being angels—but the hosts include ***all*** *of creation* being under the leadership, authority and dominion of Yahweh. Example: The Lord used the sun to stand still for Joshua to win a battle. Yahweh reserves hail and snow for the time of war. (Job 38:22-23)

The title 'Lord of Hosts' is used 282 times in Scripture. Amazingly, other titles we know well, like God our provider, healer, banner—are only used a few times in Scripture.[73] 'Lord of Hosts' is the most frequent compound term—and it's a vital aspect of God's character that we need to embrace in this new era of the Lord. As we face such giants, we need a fresh revelation of the Lord of Hosts! Interestingly, it was David the worshipper who not only had this revelation—He powerfully appropriated it against the menacing God-hater of a giant.

DAY 30

Before facing Goliath, David was trained by fighting *smaller* enemies—lions and bears. Perhaps you are being trained as you face some lions and bears. Maybe you are facing a demonic giant like Goliath. Regardless of the situation, knowing the Lord as Captain of heaven's army is critical. In these days as we are faced with anti-Christ spirits, knowing that He who is ***within us*** is bigger and greater than this Goliath provides us with great courage.

In the midst of the pressures of such battles—we can give thanks. We praise the Lord that He is bigger, stronger, wiser and more powerful than any Goliath! We give thanks because He who is greater dwells in **us.** Union with Messiah means He is in us, and we are in Him. We have access to His strength, wisdom and power.

David was quite indignant with Goliath because he knew Goliath was not defying Israel but the Lord God Himself. 'Who does Goliath think he is to challenge the Captain of heaven's army?'

David had spent his life singing to the Lord with his harp. It was his habit to give thanks. Praise changes our perspective. We see God for who He really is. As we praise, the fear of demonic giants melts. The day of battle was not too hard for David because he was a lover and worshipper of God. David knew the Lord of Hosts and trusted Him.

The only safe way to approach our giants is to know the Lord of Hosts, know He is fighting for us, and He lives within us! Hebrews 13:6 assures us; *'The Lord is my helper; I will not fear. What can man do to me?'* (NKJV)

- Victory is dependent upon His strength, not ours.
- He is greater than our enemy. The army He commands includes ***all*** of the creation. He made them all and has authority over them all!
- He dwells ***in*** us!

ACTIVATION

- What situations do you face that are too big for you to handle?
- Are there any giants threatening you today, whereby you could really do with the help of the Lord of Hosts?
- Name them.
- Do you need a fresh and vibrant revelation of the Lord of Hosts? Ask Holy Spirit to come and teach you today.
- Now lift your overwhelming circumstances to the Lord and pray in the name of the Lord of Hosts.

PRAYER

Lord of Hosts, God of the heavenly army, captain of all the hosts, God of Israel; I thank You for Your power and strength that can defeat any and every giant I am facing. You are greater than every Goliath that seeks to dishonour, mock and insult Your great name. I thank You that ***nothing*** in my life is too big or too powerful for You! Your power and authority are greater than any enemy trying to rob, kill and destroy me. I thank You that You remove the head of the giant I face. As You remove its head and authority, let Your name be glorified and exalted in the earth. Amen

Spend time praising Him because nothing you face is beyond His power.

---

71. Genesis 6:4
72. Numbers 13:33
73. Jehovah Jireh (provider) is used 2 times. Jehovah Rapha (healer) is used 3 times. Jehovah Nissi (banner) is used 6 times.

DAY 31

All Things Work Together for Good

'And we know that all things work together for good to those who love God, to those who are the called according to His purpose.' (Romans 8:28 NKJV)

'I will give all my thanks to you, Lord, for you make everything right in the end. I will sing my highest praise to the God of the Highest Place!' (Psalm 7:17 TPT)

The Lord's promise is for a good ending. But how often do we doubt this? There are some situations we face when a good outcome does not look possible. Some situations leave us wondering if we will even survive.

Thanksgiving and praise are based on our trust in, and our surrender to Him. He has the ability to turn a disaster into a miracle. Expressions of gratitude are an act of faith. They are not based on what we currently see or feel. Rather, praise is based on who *He is* and our love for Him. Our trust is in His ability to see a much bigger picture than we can. He has our best interests at heart. So even if things look sad and bad, we can trust Him to take our bad, turn it around and create a good solution.

One night when I was feeling my life had shattered into pieces, I had a picture of a brilliant artist in a junkyard. The artist collected all the bits and pieces that others had considered broken trash and useless. The artist took the discarded pieces and skilfully made something new and amazing from all the bits. With the revelation of Jesus being the greatest artist re-creating junk, I spent the next hour handing to Him all the broken pieces of my life. The next morning, I was shocked to receive a detailed message from a friend who was going through a horrendous devastation. All that the Lord had comforted me with I was now able to minister to my friend!

The Lord is the great Creator. He can make something beautiful out of our broken pieces. The Japanese art called Kintsugi takes broken pieces of pottery and puts them back together with liquid gold. These jars begin with broken pieces but are turned into exquisite and valuable pieces of art. For the Lord to turn our mess into a message, we must give Him the pieces. When we give them to Him, His glory pours into the brokenness to create something beautiful, exquisite and valuable. Nothing is wasted.

The titles of many Psalms, and the subsequent songs, provide powerful examples of King David being brutally honest about circumstances, but simultaneously trusting the Lord. Psalm 7 is titled, 'Song for a Slandered Soul'[74]. Slander by Cush had shredded David's reputation and hopes. Yet David's song begins by him expressing trust in the Lord; 'In You I take refuge' (Psalm 7:1 CJB). When trouble and disappointments come, unless we turn to the Lord first, we will never be able to believe for a good outcome.

In Psalm 62 David encourages us to tell Yahweh all our troubles. 'Pour out your heart before Him.' (Psalm 62:8 NKJV) Turning our soul to the Lord may include honest venting about everything impacting our thoughts, feelings and decisions. It's okay; He can handle it—in fact—He already knows! Most of us have no difficulty pouring out our heart to a close friend. They may not have a solution, but a caring ear is therapeutic. *The Passion Translation* renders Psalm 23 as the Lord is my 'best friend' rather than the usual 'my shepherd'.

David concludes Psalm 7 with gratitude. Yahweh caused David's troubles to boomerang on his enemy. In the end, everything was made right.

We often quote Romans 8:28 and forget the conditions. The promise is for those who love God with all their heart and who seek to obey Him. Jesus said if we love Him, we will obey Him. Giving thanks is God's will. Gratitude is an act of love, faith and obedience. For everything to work together for good, we must trust in God's goodness. Then, giving thanks becomes a key to unlock circumstances. Even if the situation itself doesn't change, our attitude to it will. Sometimes, that is all that needs to change.

In Psalm 7, King David adhered to those conditions by praising the Lord in the midst of his grief. David trusted God and expected His help.

But we should not delay our praise until we see breakthrough. In the midst of our fog—praise Him!

Yes, some circumstances of life are perplexing and we will only understand them in eternity. Hindsight regarding previous situations often gives us perfect 20/20 vision. 'Oh yes, the Lord had the best plans after all!'

Regardless of how things turn out for us or not, He knows things we don't. He holds the beginning and the end in His hands. He has your best interests at heart. We can only love, trust and obey Him.

ACTIVATION

1. Consider your circumstances. Bring them honestly to the Lord—as you would to a close friend.
2. Confess to the Lord any fear or expectation imbedded deep in your soul where you doubt He has the best plan for you. Again, be honest.
3. Read aloud: 'For I know the thoughts that I think toward you, says the Lord, thoughts of peace and not of evil, to give you a future and a hope. Then you will call upon Me and go and pray to Me, and I will listen to you.' (Jeremiah 29:11-12 NKJV)
4. Thank Him for His deep care for you by praying the Scripture in a personalised way.

PRAYER

Based on Psalm 16:5, 7-11 from *The Passion Translation*, pray this prayer of surrender, trust, gratitude and praise.

Holy and righteous Father, I thank You for Your love for me.

'I leave my destiny and its timing in Your hands...The way You counsel and correct me makes me praise You more, for Your whispers in the night give me wisdom, showing me what to do next...Because You are close to me and always available, my confidence will never be shaken...For You will not abandon me to the realm of death...For You bring me a continual revelation of resurrection life...' Amen

Give Him thanks for the good plan He has for your life.

74. Heading in *The Passion Translation*

DAY 32

Living Water

'If anyone drinks the living water I give them, they will never thirst again and will be forever satisfied! For when you drink the water I give you it becomes a gushing fountain of the Holy Spirit, springing up and flooding you with endless life!' (John 4:14 TPT)

'And he showed me a pure river of water of life, clear as crystal, proceeding from the throne of God and of the Lamb. In the middle of its street, and on either side of the river, was the tree of life, which bore twelve fruits, each tree yielding its fruit every month. The leaves of the tree were for the healing of the nations.' (Revelation 22:1-3 NKJV)

Water is vital for life— both physically and spiritually.

The human body is about 60% water. Without water we die. In the deserts of Israel and outback Australia, dehydration can kill you very quickly. So too spiritually—our need for living water is even greater.

Personally, water is my happy place. It does not matter if it's an ocean, river, lake, a swimming pool, a bathtub or a spa. When I am in, on, or around water—I get refreshed, commune better with the Lord and get more revelation. The irony is that we live 200 kms inland away from the coast!

Australia is a large, dry continent. A commercial jet takes around 6 hours to fly from north to south. Driving the same distance can take a week or more. The terrain is subject to severe drought, fire, and then floods when the rains come.

My husband Laurence grew up on a wheat and sheep property in Western Victoria, and like other farming families and communities in Australia, rain is like liquid gold. Lack of water not only affects crops and animals, the landscape, income and morale suffer from lack of water.

Central Australia has an extraordinary water system called Lake Eyre; it covers one sixth of our continent. It relies on rivers in the North to flood and this only occurs every decade or so. Yet when it fills, Lake Eyre is a spectacle from the air and it restores vegetation, fish and bird life.

Lack of spiritual water in our soul can be as dangerous as the severest drought or desert. Just like the Australian landscape, living water revives the human spirit. Yeshua promised water that would never cease and would quench the most parched tongue. He spoke of the fountain of the Holy Spirit.

When David was chased by King Saul, he hid out in the vicinity of Ein Gedi. The steep desert terrain is near the Dead Sea where the climate is extremely hot and dry. But after walking a while, you discover a refreshing waterfall. No wonder David wrote, *'As the deer pants for the water so my soul longs after You'*. Our souls can also die from lack of Holy Spirit water.

Psalm 46 begins by David stating that God is a strong refuge, a safe place for us in the midst of turbulent times. David's storm was hiding from a crazed King Saul. Ein Gedi was his hiding place.

But in verse 4, David seems to make an odd or out of place reference to God's River. '*There is a river whose streams shall make glad the city of God, the holy place of the tabernacle...*'(Psalm 46:4 NKJV) David's Psalm is stating that it doesn't matter if you are in the midst of a political or physical storm, an earthquake or volcano; God's river, coming from His throne, provides 'joy and delight' to His people. The Lord is not just a safe place during chaos—He is also our joy!

Holy Spirit rivers are filled with life. In heaven, either side of the river is the tree of life. They produce great fruit, and the leaves of the trees bring healing for nations!

Hence David concluded the Psalm, '*Be still, and know that I am God; I will be exalted among the nations, I will be exalted in the earth! The Lord of hosts is with us...*' (Psalm 46:10-11 NKJV)

Worshipping the Lord in His Presence, praying and singing in tongues are powerful ways to get into the River of Life. Are you feeling spiritually parched or dehydrated? Get into His river, where living water flows from His throne to revive, heal, restore, and revitalise. In the midst of chaos, get into His river and you will know rest and shalom.

ACTIVATION

1. When one goes for a swim in a dry place, you quickly leave your gear on the side and plunge in. Place all your troubling stuff on the side—give it to Him. Spend some time splashing in His waterfall! Enjoy His refreshment—knowing He is looking after the stuff you left on the dry ground.
2. Thank Him for a fresh drink from His well of salvation to satisfy your soul. Total satisfaction.

PRAYER

Righteous Father, I thank You for the gift of the Holy Spirit. Your living water is hydrating and refreshing my thirsty soul.

I thank You for the living water of Your Word to wash, cleanse me and refresh me.

I thank You for the river flowing from Your throne—with healing and restoration. Amen

Continue to give Him thanks for living water.

Pray and sing in the Spirit—and enjoy His river.

Journal your experience with Him today.

DAY 33

Seven Spirits of Fire

'I will not leave you orphans...but the Helper, the Holy Spirit, whom the Father will send in My name, He will teach you all things' (John 14:18-26 NKJV)

'Seven lamps of fire *were burning before the throne,* ***which are the seven Spirits of God.****' (Revelation 4:5 NKJV)*

'... in the midst of the throne and of the four living creatures, and in the midst of the elders, stood ***a Lamb as though it had been slain****, having* ***seven horns*** *and* ***seven eyes, which are the seven Spirits of God*** *sent out into all the earth.' (Revelation 5:6 NKJV)*

'The Spirit of the Lord shall rest upon Him, The Spirit of wisdom and understanding, The Spirit of counsel and might, The Spirit of knowledge and of the fear of the Lord.' (Isaiah 11:2 NKJV)

As Yeshua prepared to return to heaven, He promised His disciples He would not leave them without help. He would not abandon them. The Holy Spirit would be present on earth to provide comfort, help, and the miraculous dynamite power the disciples would need.[75]

The Holy Spirit was sent to help us through life—that includes to help us stop grumbling! The ministry of the Holy Spirit is powerful and necessary to sanctify us, teach us and help us praise.

The Church was birthed at Pentecost with a ***sound*** from heaven. Sound and praise are always together. The sound at Pentecost was the wind of the Spirit descending as tongues of fire. The tongues of fire came from heaven where seven flames burn before the throne of God. These are the seven Spirits of God.[76]

The seven Spirits are not seven *different* Spirits, but rather seven characteristics of the Holy Spirit. If we describe the characteristics of someone we know well, we likely list many characteristics of that person. For example, we may say the person is kind, has a sense of humour, is trustworthy and so on.

The seven characteristics of the Spirit of God are:

1. Wisdom
2. Understanding
3. Counsel
4. Might (power, strength)
5. Knowledge
6. Awe and reverence (fear of the Lord)
7. The Presence of the Lord / Voice of Prophecy[77]

On the day of Pentecost, it was the fullness (revealed by number 7[78]) of the Spirit that fell upon the disciples. The disciples received all seven attributes of the Holy Spirit. And all seven were demonstrated in the book of Acts. Now, these seven characteristics help us in our walk with Him. They help us to see God in our circumstances, grant us revelation and insight, and help us to give thanks for miracles as we await them by faith!

The seven spirits are described as the seven horns and seven eyes of Jesus the Lamb of God.[79] Horns represent power and authority, while eyes speak of prophetic vision. Tongues of fire ignite passion, refine and purify. The fire, horns and eyes help us personally, but also as we intercede for cities and nations.

The seven Spirits help us see our personal stuff from heaven's perspective and release His power and authority as we praise. The seven Spirits help us to see the spiritual battles we face and give us divine strategies—many times in worship. The seven Spirits enable us to see what He is doing in nations so we can align and partner with Him.

Heavenly Language for Perfect Praise

A key manifestation of the Holy Spirit at Pentecost was the gift of tongues. The supernatural download of different languages enabled the disciples to praise God in a unique way. People from different parts of the world could hear the disciples speaking 'about the great things God has done'—in their own languages and dialects. (Acts 2:11) Without realising it, the disciples were supernaturally praising God for His miracles! Their praise went beyond their own experiences.

The Holy Spirit gift of tongues intersects with praise. Use it frequently and you will be empowered to overcome the default to grumbling.

Paul instructed the Corinthian church about the appropriate use of the gifts—especially for prayer and praise.

> *'For he who speaks in a tongue does not speak to men but to God, for no one understands him; however, in the spirit he speaks mysteries. He who* ***speaks in a tongue edifies***

> ***himself**, but he who **prophesies edifies the church**… I will pray with the spirit, and I will also pray with the understanding. I will sing with the spirit, and I will also sing with the understanding.' (1 Corinthians 14:2-4, 15 NKJV)*

Praying and singing in tongues ***edifies the individual***. However, when praying and singing in tongues, Paul concludes: 'You indeed give thanks well.' (1 Corinthians 14:17 NKJV) The Passion Translation quotes verse 15 as *'I will **sing rapturous praises in the Spirit**, but I will also sing with my mind engaged.'*

Singing in tongues is the most excellent and powerful way to give thanks to God. It is a gift from God to help us bypass our natural senses of fraught emotions and confused minds. It enables us to offer pure and beautiful praise. It is the language of heaven. When we sing in tongues our praise originates in heaven, flows through our spirit man and back to the Lord. Thus, singing in tongues is cyclical and releases rapturous praise! The Greek word *kalos* (G2570)[80] suggests these praises are beautiful, excellent, admirable, honourable, genuine, precious, valuable, pure, comforting and confirming.

I believe we often diminish what Paul was saying about tongues and its ability to strengthen our inner man and enhance our praise. Singing in tongues releases the sounds and songs of heaven. It helps us individually and corporately to quickly ascend in the Spirit. Praying and singing in tongues is under-utilised and under-appreciated in the Church today. It is a gift we need to value and stir up as we face momentous challenges in society.

ACTIVATION

1. Write down and then surrender to the Lord any tricky or tough circumstances you are facing.
2. As you lift these before the Lord, pray and sing in tongues over them.

PRAYER

Righteous Father, I am so grateful You have not abandoned me, but rather You sent Your Holy Spirit to help me, comfort, strengthen and anoint me in prayer and praise.

I thank You, Holy Spirit, for providing me with the help I need—Your wisdom, understanding, counsel, knowledge, power and strength, awe and reverence, for Your Presence and Your prophetic voice.

Thank You for Your fire to refine and inspire. Thank You for Your passion.

As I yield to You, Holy Spirit, thank You for helping me bring an offering of perfect praise. Thank You for miracles in the past. I praise You for Your *dynamos* power touching me and realising miracles today—especially the ones I can't see yet. Amen

Keep praising Him through the power and gifts of the Holy Spirit.

75. Acts 1:8 John 14-16
76. Revelation 4:5 Isaiah 11:1-3
77. The testimony of Jesus is the spirit of prophecy.
78. The number 7 in Scripture speaks of completion, fullness or perfection. 7 days of creation week; 7 Spirits of God; 7 colours of rainbow; 7 notes in music; Passover and Tabernacles go for 7 days.
79. Revelation 5:6
80. Strong's Concordance

DAY 34

Fruit of the Spirit

'When I look at you, I see how you have taken My fruit and tasted My word... Your inward life is now sprouting, bringing forth fruit. What a beautiful paradise unfolds within you...' (Song of Solomon 4:2, 13,14 TPT)

'But the fruit of the Spirit is love, joy, peace, long-suffering, kindness, goodness, faithfulness, gentleness, self-control. Against such there is no law...' (Galatians 5:22-23 NKJV)

I love fruit – especially when its fresh from our own trees or from the Australian tropics. Take the different varieties of fruit; pineapple, watermelon, passionfruit, banana, apricots, raspberries and cherries and mix them all together into a yummy fruit salad. This favourite dessert is not only delicious, but easily digested and full of nutrients. Even better with ice-cream!

Fruit of the Spirit—Who He Is

One day I was thinking about the fruits of the Spirit and realised our primary thought is often about how to grow them in us. As I mulled upon the encouragement of Psalm 34:8 to 'taste and see that the Lord is good', I had a light bulb moment—the fruit first originates with God Himself! The fruit of the Spirit is who He is. They describe His character and nature!

I realised I had been so concerned with the fruit of the Spirit being formed within me, I had forgotten to enjoy the fruit originating and radiating from Him!

Fruit Tasting

A wise farmer would include a fruit tasting as part of the decision-making process to grow fruit.

The process of Holy Spirit growing His fruits in us can be a lengthy and arduous process. Maybe it would be wise to first have a good feed on His fruit, to 'taste and see the Lord is good'. Feast on Him, enjoy and be nourished by Him. Give thanks for His yummy fruit—it's the best fruit salad!

Feasting on Him first would encourage us to then do the tough stuff needed for His fruit to grow in us; the spiritual pruning and fertilising!

> *'For everything connected with our self-life was put to death on the cross and crucified with Messiah. We must live in the Holy Spirit and follow after him.' (Galatians 5:24, 25 TPT)*

Who Eats the Fruit Formed in Us?

As we journey through the tough stuff to grow His fruit in us, other people will eat from what we produce. Who eats the fruit formed in us? Do they pick yummy fruit that is sweet and juicy or fruit that is it not ripe and even sour?

1. Many in the world, like family and friends, who have yet to feed directly on the Lord's fruit, may first discover

this exotic delicious morsel by eating the fruit we grow in our lives.

2. Rather astonishing to consider: Yeshua Himself is nourished by the fruit we grow. Read Song of Solomon: 2:13-14 and Psalm 110 in *The Passion Translation.*

The dialogue between the Bridegroom and Bride in Song of Solomon 4 confirms this idea. She eats His fruit and then His fruit grows in her. As the Bride matures, she then invites Him to 'Come taste the fruits of Your life in me.' (Song of Solomon 5:1 TPT)

In the course of the dialogue, nine fruits are mentioned. Though Song of Solomon 4 also contain botanical names of the fruits, they are very comparable to the list of fruit mentioned in Galatians 5.

Let us:

- Feast on His fruit
- Embrace the cross and permit Holy Spirit to grow His fruit in us
- Let Him feast on the fruit in us
- Let others feast on the fruit in us

ACTIVATION and PRAYER

Psalm 1:2 says to meditate on the Word of God. The Hebrew word *hagah* means to ponder, mutter, talk, study, imagine. Meditating on the Word is a bit like when we chew something over. Chew on the various mouthfuls and allow our heart and mouth to soar with gratitude to the Lord.

Meditate and chew on the fruits of the Spirit—and give thanks for the feast!

- As you taste and see, give thanks; God is love—and His love is so great its boundaries cannot be explored![81]
- As you taste and see, give thanks; the oil of joy replaces mourning, and His joy is our strength.
- As you taste and see, give thanks; Shalom guards our heart and passes all understanding!
- As you taste and see, give thanks; He is patient, perseveres and does not quit on you!
- As you taste and see, give thanks; Love is kind. He is kind even to those who are unthankful and evil.[82]
- Taste and see; His goodness and mercy are like bodyguards who follow me every day![83]
- As you taste and see, give thanks; Great is His faithfulness. Its fresh every morning and extends to all generations.[84]
- As you taste and see, give thanks; Embrace and learn from Yeshua because He is meek, and humble. He gives you rest for your soul![85]
- As you taste and see, give thanks; Yeshua demonstrated the greatest of self-control and strength of Spirit in the Garden of Gethsemane, His unfair trial and crucifixion.

Continue to speak to Him from your heart with thanksgiving.

---

81. Romans 8
82. Luke 6:35
83. Psalm 23:6
84. Lam 3:23; Psalm 119:90
85. Matthew 11:29

DAY 35

Wisdom Is Your Bodyguard!

'Wisdom is a gift from a generous God... For the Lord has a hidden storehouse of wisdom made accessible to his godly lovers. ***He becomes your personal bodyguard as you follow his ways, protecting and guarding you as you choose what is right.*** *Then you will discover all that is just, proper, and fair, and be empowered to make the right decisions as you walk into your destiny.' (Proverbs 2:6-9 TPT)*

God is generous. Amongst His bountiful gifts to us is wisdom. He has a storehouse full of wisdom ready to give to His lovers and worshippers.

Creation and Redemption are both wrapped in wisdom. Wisdom was the master craftsman at Creation (Proverbs 8:22-30). Paul's first letter to the Corinthian church begins with sixteen references to wisdom—and all about salvation.

- Yeshua Messiah is the wisdom of God. (1 Corinthians 1:24, 30)
- God's wisdom baffles human wisdom.

- God's wisdom chose to defeat the devil by Yeshua going to the cross! Man's wisdom would never consider such a strategy. (1 Corinthians 1:18-21)
- We draw our life from being in union with Him. He is our wisdom, holiness, redemption. (1 Corinthians 1:30; 3:23)
- Faith is established by trusting God's power. (1 Corinthians 2:5)
- God's wisdom brings us into glory! (1 Corinthians 2:7) If the rulers of this world had known this fact, they would never have crucified Yeshua.

God's wisdom touches our personal lives—it created a plan for our life and is like a personal bodyguard protecting us from danger. (Proverbs 2:6-9; 8:12)

Wrong choices can ruin lives. Bad choices create havoc, heartache and regrets. Wisdom guards and helps us to make right choices—even creative ones! Ignoring and even despising wisdom is akin to flirting with death. (Proverbs 8:36) As our personal bodyguard, wisdom protects us from making foolish decisions. Wise choices enable us to walk into our God-given destiny. Wise choices enable us to be fruitful. Wise choices bring blessings and favour into family life, in business, the workplace, in churches, in communities, in any form of leadership.

Just as wisdom was active in the creation of the world, we can trust He will answer when we ask for wisdom. His answers are likely to be creative and out of the box! The Lord is doing so many amazing things in the world today—and many are through very creative strategies!

When we are faced with difficult choices, it is wonderful to consider—God gives wisdom as a gift to those who love Him! We don't have to earn it, beg for it, or be super spiritual.

1. Give thanks—and worship!

> *The **starting point** for **acquiring wisdom** is to be **consumed with awe** as you worship Jehovah-God.' (Proverbs 9:10 TPT)*

We begin to get wisdom through worship. Often translated the 'fear of the Lord', this phrase does not mean we are intimidated; rather, we are in awe of God. Bowing in awe before Him is actually one of the definitions of the Hebrew and Greek words for worship. As we discover who He is, we bow, we worship, we get further revelation and bow and worship some more. Being consumed with awe is not just a once only event, it is a process, a journey.

It is on this journey of gratitude and worship we acquire wisdom. The wisdom of God is more valuable than gold, leads us into righteousness, and brings peace into our lives. Once on this journey you can begin to ask for more wisdom.

2. Ask God for Wisdom

> *'If any of you **needs wisdom** to know **what you should do**, you should **ask God**, and He will give it to you. God is generous to everyone and doesn't find fault with them. When you ask for something, don't have any doubts.' (James 1:5,6 GW)*

Ask and don't doubt. Father is good, very good. He only gives good gifts in response to our requests. (Matthew 7:8-11) When we ask for wisdom, be assured, His answer and His wisdom will be good. If wisdom could assist creation and salvation in such an amazing way—imagine what it can do to help you!

ACTIVATION

1. Write down and name every circumstance where you are currently needing to make decisions

___

___

___

2. Lift these decisions to the Lord with prayer and thanksgiving for His wisdom.

PRAYER

Lord God Almighty, I thank You for Your storehouse of wisdom that is filled with valuable treasures![86] I appreciate Your wisdom as seen in Creation, in Yeshua, in His cross, in choices You have made. Hallelujah, Your wisdom is far above the wisdom of man! I bless You. Yeshua is the face of wisdom.

I am so grateful You have given wisdom to me as a bodyguard, protecting me from dangerous paths and wrong choices. I thank You for wisdom's help to make good and honourable choices. I am grateful, I can trust Your wisdom to not lead me astray, but to help me choose the right path. Thank You, Father, Your wisdom helps me fulfil the destiny You have written in my book. Amen

Praise Him for His wisdom directing and guarding your circumstances.

Praise Him. Worship Him. Enjoy His awesome Presence.

---

86. Proverbs 8:19-21 James 3:17-18

DAY 36

Gratitude for People in Your Life

(Part 1) Gifts

*'Always **give thanks** to Father God for **every person** He brings into your life in the name of our Lord Jesus Christ.' (Ephesians 5:20 TPT)*

When we are in grumbling mode, it contaminates the lens of how we see people. When we are in the modus operandi of grumbling, the faults and weaknesses in our nearest and dearest seem to get larger and larger and more irritating.

Worse still, out grumbling infects the atmosphere around us. It can certainly touch, discourage and wound others. It certainly creates an unpleasant and unhealthy environment.

On the other hand, if our modus operandi is gratitude, we then see the best in people. We see their strengths and gifts. We realise these people are a blessing to us. The atmosphere changes and life is much sweeter.

Consider ***all*** the people in your life. Not just the ones you like, but all of them. How do you see them? Can you give thanks for all of them? Do you see them as created in the image of God and loved by Him? Do you see each one as a person Jesus died for?

Do you see each person in Your life as ***a gift*** given to you by our loving Father?

You mean everybody? Well—yes!

Many people in our circle of life bring an automatic smile to our face and joy to our heart. But what about the people who are challenging or make us feel a little uncomfortable?

Over today and tomorrow, consider ***all*** the people in your life as gifts. However, we will place them into two categories. Today we will consider those who bring you great joy. Tomorrow we will consider the challenging ones. Some people will fit into both categories. Well, you can go ahead and give thanks for them twice!

Giving Thanks for People who Bring you Joy.

For today, let's just consider all the people who make your life enjoyable. Consider those who bring a smile to your face, a song to your heart, and those who help you through life. Sometimes we would not get through certain situations without the help, encouragement and prayers of a particular family member, friend or colleague. See them as a gift from God. Identify them as a blessing.

There have been times I have needed – and have recognised this need – to feel the heavenly Father's arms in the here and now, in the flesh. I have been blessed on those occasions to experience my husband's arms as representative of Father's arms of unconditional love.

Father knows every *need* you have, as distinct from your *wants*. He provides answers for all our needs. Sometimes we don't recognise our real need or the provision for it.

Today is your opportunity to consider, and maybe discover, the special people He has provided as a gift to help your life.

ACTIVATION

1. Think about and then write down the names of five people in your life who you consider are real gifts from God. These will be people who make your life better and life would be really tough without them. These five people may be family, friends, colleagues, ministry partners, work colleagues, business associates, or health care workers. There is space below to write in your answers. Put each name on a separate line, because there are further questions to write beside their names. You may be able to name more than five people. For now, start with five, and you can add more later. As you write your list of names, think about the people who frequently bless you and those for whom you can truly say, 'Thank You, Lord, for bringing this special person into my life'. Go ahead, list the names of God's gifts to you.

2. Now, beside the name of each person, write down 1-3 things they do that causes you to smile. What is it about them that makes you so glad they are in your life?

3. Have you ever told them how much they bless you?

Person #1 ______________________________

____

____

Person #2 ____

____

____

Person #3 ____

____

____

Person #4 ____

____

____

Person #5 ____

____

____

PRAYER

Your list above is the basis of today's prayer. Give thanks for each person, one at a time.

Lord, I thank You for (name them)__________________.

I am so blessed to have__________________in my life because he / she is a precious gift from You. I especially appreciate that they (list the 1-3 things you have written) ______________________.

Now pray a special prayer of blessing over: ____________________________.

Ask the Holy Spirit for a practical and beautiful way to express your gratitude to the person.

DAY 37

Gratitude for People in Your Life (Part 2) Making Pearls

'Always give thanks to Father God for every person He brings into your life in the name of our Lord Jesus Christ.' (Ephesians 5:20 TPT)

'The kingdom of heaven is like a merchant who was searching for fine pearls.' (Matthew 13:45 GW)

Yesterday we discovered God has given you many gifts—they are the people in your life. As you considered key people who bring you great joy, I am sure you discovered more treasures than you realised. No doubt your heart glowed as you gave thanks.

Today we are going to give thanks for the people who appear to have a special sandpaper ministry! You know, those precious ones who rub us the wrong way. It is so easy to see their faults. We could easily and gladly itemise all the things they need to fix, to remove their scratchy bits! And yes, we can easily grizzle and complain about them.

Some people from yesterday's list may actually appear again today. Some folk really do bless us, yet there are times they are a great irritant. Maybe it's tougher to see this aspect of your relationship with them as also being a gift from the Lord!

Whether we see a person as a gift or an irritant, we need to ask the same questions as yesterday.

Can you give thanks for them? '*You mean I have to give thanks for the ones who rub me up the wrong way? You mean I have to be grateful for the one who always criticises me*?' How is it possible that these too are a gift from God? Are they not also created in the image of God and loved by Him? Didn't Jesus die for them too?

Making of Precious Pearls

Consider the process that nature uses to produce precious pearls.

Every time an irritating speck afflicts an oyster, it protects itself by coating the irritation with a mineral substance. These irritations can be as simple as a grain of sand—small but irritating to the oyster. Irritation after irritation is covered. It reminds me of the Proverb that says, 'Love covers a multitude of sins.' The oyster produces layers of mineral substance over each irritation until a pearl is formed.

There are some people in our lives that force us to press hard into God for His grace, mercy and forgiveness. Maybe some of these people have caused you to see things in yourself you didn't see before. It is said that the things that anger us about others are often the very things that angers us about ourselves. Sometimes

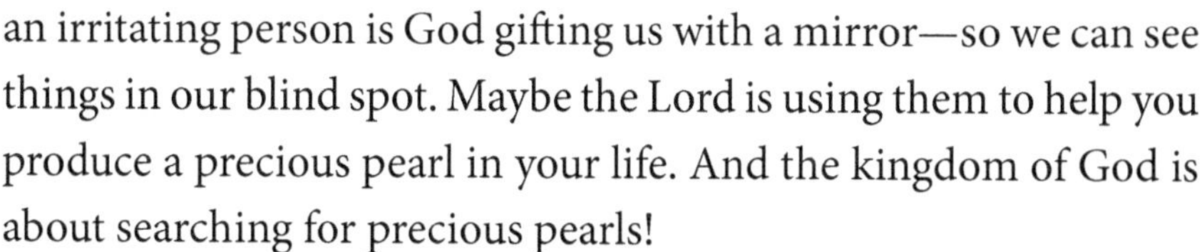

an irritating person is God gifting us with a mirror—so we can see things in our blind spot. Maybe the Lord is using them to help you produce a precious pearl in your life. And the kingdom of God is about searching for precious pearls!

Your choice today is to grumble about these dear people or to let His pearl grow in you.

ACTIVATION

Grow some spiritual pearls today!

1. Write down the names of the people in your life who are a challenge, even an irritant. They may be a spouse, children, relatives, friends, work colleagues, business associate, co-workers. They may be someone who you wrote down yesterday because they bless you, but there are some things they do that drive you crazy. Like yesterday, keep one line for each person.

2. List 1-3 things they bring to your life that God is using to refine you, grow you, develop and mature you. Yes, you can write down the irritation—but only if you can identify how that irritant is helping you to grow a precious pearl.

3. When you have completed your list, pray with gratitude for each person. As you do, ask the Lord to bless the person.

Person #1 ____________________________________

____

____

Person #2 ____________________________________

____

____

Person #3 ____________________________________

____

____

Person #4 ____________________________________

____

____

Person #5 ____________________________________

____

____

Prayer

Lord, I thank You for ______________________. I recognise ______________________ is a gift from You because he / she challenges me by: ______________________.

I thank You that each time I extend Your grace, Your mercy and Your forgiveness, Your love is covering a multitude of sins and a precious pearl is growing in my life.

Now I ask You to especially bless__________________ today. Amen

DAY 38

Spirit Wind and Glory Light!

'The earth was without form, and void; and darkness was on the face of the deep. And the Spirit of God was hovering over the face of the waters. Then God said, 'Let there be light'; and there was light...' (Genesis 1:2–4 NKJV)

'And the Lord God formed man of the dust of the ground, and breathed into his nostrils the breath of life; and man became a living being.' (Genesis 2:7 NKJV)

'Jesus spoke to them again, saying, 'I AM the light of the world. He who follows Me shall not walk in darkness, but have the light of life'. (John 8:12 NKJV)

'So Jesus said to them... As the Father has sent Me, I also send you.' And when He had said this, He breathed on them, and said to them, 'Receive the Holy Spirit.' (John 20:21-22 NKJV)

'Let him smother me with kisses—his Spirit-kiss divine.' (Song of Solomon 1:2 TPT)

Creation Brooding

In the beginning, as per Genesis 1, there was chaos and disorder. Many believe this occurred after Lucifer led a rebellion, taking out one third of the angels. Over all the darkness, the Spirit of God hovered, brooded and breathed life. Movement of air is the fundamentals of sound. Wind blowing through trees creates a sound. Breath going through a flute or trumpet creates a distinct sound. The breath of God releases Holy Spirit movement and sound. On the day of Pentecost a sound of a mighty wind from heaven blew into the upper room. The sound released movement, or a move of God. The breath of God will awaken any mess, chaos and dysfunction in our lives. Invite Him to do that for you today.

Then God spoke! The sound of His voice singing over the mess and the power of His creative Word brought forth light. Creation and divine order began with the Spirit breath and glory light. The breath of all mankind comes from God.[87] The heavens were made by the breath of His mouth.[88] Life comes from His breath. Life is the light of men.[89] Jesus is the light!

Adamic Kiss

At first reading, the words of the Shulamite Bride in Song of Solomon 1:2 may seem a little strange, even weird! But it is poetry! 'Let Him smother me with kisses—His Spirit-kiss divine.'

When I was training for my senior certificate in swimming, I had to learn life-saving skills. Giving mouth-to-mouth resuscitation to a drowning person means the rescuer breathes air into the mouth of the one who was drowning. It was aptly called 'the kiss of life.'

And like in Sleeping Beauty, the prince, our Creator and bridegroom King—kisses us to break the curse, to save us from death and awaken us to His love. The commentary from *The Passion*

Translation says; 'This Spirit kiss is what made Adam, the man of clay, into a living expression of God. Dust and deity met when the Maker kissed His Spirit wind into Adam. The Word of God is the kiss from the mouth of our Beloved, breathing upon us the revelation of His love.'[90]

Similarly, after His resurrection, Yeshua appeared to His disciples and breathed on them.[91] Linguistically, it is similar to God breathing on dirt to form Adam. Jesus breathed on the disciples for them to receive resurrection life—the very glory of the Father and Holy Spirit breath that had raised Jesus from the dead.[92] Ten days later, heaven released the wind of the Spirit to revolutionise earth!

Let There Be Light!

At creation, God breathed on darkness. His breath became words. Light was released. The light of Yeshua is powerful in prayer and praise.

Teenagers provide many challenges to parents and teachers alike. In my teaching profession I predominantly taught teenagers. But the situations of our own children touch us deeper. In the midst of some teenage 'darkness', the Lord taught me to pray and praise according to Genesis 1:1-3. I saw dramatic results. What I thought would take years took just days. Regardless of how much darkness surrounds you, invite Holy Spirit to breathe on it and the light of Yeshua to dispel it!

Yeshua is the light. His light is so bright that the New Jerusalem has no need for electricity, sun or moon, because the glory of God, the Lamb, is its light! (Revelation 21:23) Natural light is also a gift from God.

- Light removes darkness.
- Light brings warmth, health and growth. (Vitamin D and photosynthesis.)[93]

- Light exposes what is hidden by darkness.[94] It provides safety so our feet do not trip on unseen obstacles.[95]
- Light is an armour,[96] protecting us from lies and deception and demonic darkness. While praying, I saw a soldier dressed in armour. Sunshine and glory reflected from his shield was so bright that the approaching enemy was blinded!
- Light is fast. Its frequencies are faster than sound.
- Light fills the kingdom of God—darkness is the realm of the devil.[97]
- God's light brings us into true unity.[98] Like a powerful oxy torch and laser beam, His light separates, heals and welds our broken pieces together.

More than ever we need the creative breath, the glory light and Resurrection life of Jesus!

Cycle of Breath and Light

God's breath and light are cyclical akin to the water cycle. No wonder everything that has breath is called to praise! [99]

Rain falls from the clouds. Water on earth is evaporated by the sunlight. More clouds are formed by moisture in the air, and more rain falls. A similar process takes place in the cycle of God's breath.

He breathes His life into us. We use our breath to praise Him—like we are breathing on Him. Praise ascends. The Son who is light draws it up and receives it into heaven. The Spirit breathes on it and it again falls on us, bringing more life, more joy, more blessings! When everything that has breath praises Him, we continue the cycle of the light and breath of God!

His breath gives and sustains life. His resurrection life is a breath of fresh air, especially when life removes the wind from our sails! Every time we read and absorb the Word of God into our heart, it is like a kiss from heaven.

His Breath and Glory Light Destroy the Evil One

> *'The lawless one will be revealed, whom the Lord will consume with the breath of His mouth and destroy with the brightness of His coming'. (2 Thessalonians 2:8 NKJV)*

His breath vaporises the enemy! When Jesus, who is light, appears in His brightness, the evil one is destroyed, rendered useless and made to vanish. This Scripture is in the context of the anti-Christ or lawless one! Be encouraged. When overwhelming evil is rampant—the Lord's breath and His light consume the enemy.

Without His breath and His light, we do not live—physically or spiritually.

ACTIVATION

We have so much to thank Him for today!

As you praise, there are two questions to ask the Holy Spirit.

1. What part of my life needs the creative resurrection breath of God?
2. What part of my life needs His glory light to expose darkness?

Write His answers in your journal.

Now lift them to Him with thanksgiving and with the prayer below.

PRAYER

Let the old hymn be your prayer today: 'Breathe on me breathe of God'.[100]

1. Breathe on me, breath of God: fill me with life anew,
That I may love as You have loved, and do as You would do.

2. Breathe on me, breath of God, until my heart is pure,
Until my will is one with Yours, to do and to endure.

3. Breathe on me, breath of God; fulfil my heart's desire,
Until this earthly part of me, glows with Your heavenly fire.

Precious Father, I thank You for Your life-sustaining breath today. I receive Your 'kisses' with joy. Your breath is moving over my darkness. Your light is penetrating, removing and ruling over all chaos in my life![101] Amen

As you continue to praise Him, also decree, 'Let there be light'.

---

87. Job 12:10
88. Psalm 33:6
89. John 1:4
90. The Passion Translation footnote (c) Song of Solomon 1:2
91. John 20
92.Romans 6:4; Romans 8:11
93. Vitamin D is a chemical needed to strengthen bones and the immune system. It is produced in the body when exposed to sunlight. Plants and trees use photosynthesis to make food and oxygen from sunlight, and carbon monoxide.
94. 1 Corinthians 4:5
95. John 12:35
96. Romans 13:12
97 Acts 26:18 Ephesians 5:8; 6:12
98. 1 John 1: 6-7 TPT
99. Psalm 150
100. "Breathe on Me Breathe of God", written by Edwin Hatch 1878 "He reached down into my darkness to rescue me!
101. Psalm 18:16 TPT; Psalm 93:3-4 TPT

DAY 39

Heavenly Lawyer, Intercessor, High Priest

'...we do not have a High Priest who cannot sympathize with our weaknesses, but was in all points tempted as we are, yet without sin.' (Hebrews 4:15 NKJV)

'Likewise the Spirit also helps in our weaknesses. For we do not know what we should pray for as we ought, but the Spirit Himself makes intercession for us with groanings which cannot be uttered.' (Romans 8:26 NKJV)

God has provided us with the most qualified High Priest, intercessor, and lawyer to be found in the universe —Yeshua!

Heavenly Attorney

The devil accuses God's people 24/7, and our world is increasing in vitriolic litigations. Having Yeshua as our heavenly attorney is a great relief. He is compassionate, understanding, full of grace and smart. He is wisdom personified and through Him the invisible and visible worlds were created.

His unique ability is because He understands the weakness and frailty of the human condition. He does not present us to the Father through a filter of aloof judgement, but though painful identification.

The devil often adds condemnation and shame to his accusations. When we agree with the devil, we become our own worst witness against ourselves! Unlike us, Yeshua did not come to earth to condemn. He came to give life. (John 3:17)

Intercessor

When Moses was interceding during the battle with the Amalekites, his arms got tired. Aaron and Hur held up the arms of Moses until victory was secured. Jesus as High Priest and Holy Spirit hold our arms up in intercession until victory is secured.

Yeshua intercedes for us at the right hand of the Father with compassion, understanding, sensitivity, and kindness. He was tempted like us—yet He overcame and did not sin. He understands our frailty, yet He also shows us that overcoming is possible. He is the perfect High Priest, advocate, intercessor. His understanding does not cause Him to excuse or wink at sin, for He is righteous. Nor does he condemn us to destroy us. Rather, His kind understanding embraces us even in the midst of failure. The purpose of His kindness is to restore our hope and to lift us up so we too can overcome.

The description of the Holy Spirit's intercession suggests travail. His prayer is deep and comprehensive—far greater than we could pray for ourselves! Praying with groaning is akin to the pain and sorrow of childbirth. Travail is so deep, words fail. Travail is bringing something to birth in the Spirit.

An attorney is hired when an accusation has been made. The attorney defends their client. A prayer 'attorney' defends us against an accusation. Prayer that is travail is birthing something and suggests taking new ground, thus overcoming resistance to destiny. Over our lifetime we will at times need travail and at other times a prayer attorney. Defence and offence are both needed for victory.

What an astonishing thought—Holy Spirit and Yeshua pray for us! Thank Him for His prayers for you today!

ACTIVATION AND PRAYER

Spend time giving thanks.

Thank You, Lord, for understanding me. I am so grateful that You know my personality and every detail about me even before my conception. You know my family, my heritage, my DNA, and the circumstances around my birth and upbringing. I am so grateful that none of it is a surprise or a shock to You. You love me despite my history—and none of it is too hard for You to redeem! Amen

Keep praising Him.

Loving Father, I am so grateful that You see, You know and You care about every current circumstance that I face now. As I lift these up before You, I am blown away that Yeshua and Holy Spirit are already interceding for me. Their prayer is helping me to find the right path through the maze of iniquity, sorrow, injustice, and temptation. I am humbly grateful that You who made me are praying for me, singing over me and believing for me. Amen

- Now thank Father for providing such a highly qualified and compassionate High-Priest, advocate, intercessor as Yeshua!
- Bless Yeshua for His willingness to put aside His majesty, so He could identify with human frailty.
- Thank Holy Spirit for understanding your deep, deepest need and praying the perfect prayer for your situation.

Thank the Lord that He is cheering for you—urging you on to finish well.

DAY 40

Provision for Every Need

'And my God shall supply all your need according to His riches in glory by Christ Jesus.' (Philippians 4:19 NKJV)

Sometimes our needs are beyond our own resources!

How do we respond? Pray, beg or complain? What about thanksgiving?

The Lord really taught us on this one when we had a desperate need for a different car. We were not asking for a brand new car; simply to shift from a sedan to a solid and reliable station wagon, but we did not have the money for it.

We began the journey according to our old nature. We asked, we begged, we reminded God of our need. Nothing changed. The pressure mounted and intensified.

I had just written my first book on worship and was in process of publishing it. Prior to writing, the Lord had changed my life through thanksgiving. He then showed us we were to take a road trip around Australia (thousands of kilometres), to release the book.

We would be away for 3 months and needed clothes for four of us and for the winter and summer climates across Australia.

Our children were in primary school, so they had to take their school work, as well as some toys to keep them occupied in the car. We had camping gear, and of course the books. Our existing vehicle was way too small and unsuited for the conditions of the Australian outback. Our departure date kept looming closer and closer and we needed a more suitable vehicle.

We prayed. We fasted. We sought the Lord. We begged. It seemed I had too easily forgotten the previous lesson of giving thanks! Then the Lord spoke to both Laurence and me on the same day: 'Give thanks for the provision'. The Lord reminded us both to give thanks in everything. He reminded us that He provides all our needs. We needed to stop begging and shift to thanksgiving.

So we began to thank God for His call on our lives. We thanked Him our need was not yet fulfilled and we were being tested! It was not a long or elaborate prayer—but it was from the heart, and it was in obedience to His direction. Immediately we both had peace about the situation. After that, we gave thanks together every day. The days turned to weeks, and the deadline kept getting closer. We continued to give thanks and the peace remained in our hearts.

One day while chatting with a relative, an offer was made to buy our existing vehicle. While that would help, there would still be a shortfall. But it was encouraging. We continued to give thanks. We also began looking for a suitable vehicle with a friend who was a mechanic. He found us a great buy, but we were still short. We continued to give thanks.

When the transactions took place, finances supernaturally increased and we had enough for the new vehicle. We left on our trip at the appointed time, in a vehicle that fitted everything, and it didn't give us any problems during the whole 3-month journey!

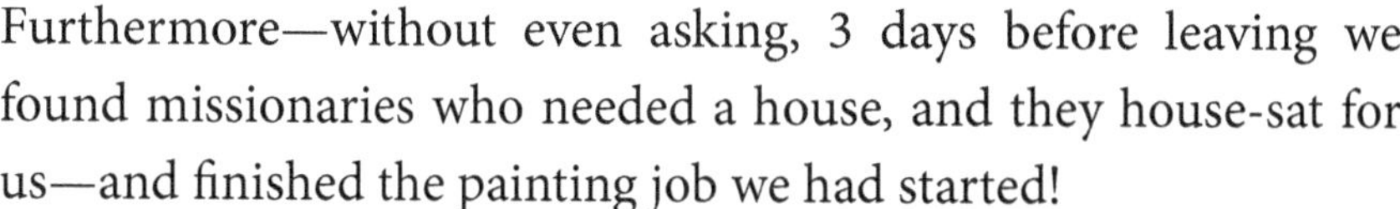

Furthermore—without even asking, 3 days before leaving we found missionaries who needed a house, and they house-sat for us—and finished the painting job we had started!

What pressing need do you have in your life? What do you need that is necessary for you to fulfil God's call in your life? What is missing that stops you from being whole and complete? Try to be honest before the Lord.

His glory realm is full of provision. His glory contains everything we need. Needs are not restricted to finances. It can be healing of bodies and minds. It may be a relationship that is in need of healing and restoration.

It was the glory of the Father that raised Jesus from the dead. (Romans 6:4) Dead things, people and circumstances can come to life from His glory. Don't try to work out 'how' He will do it. All we have to do is give Him thanks for the provision in His glory. Keep thanking Him, and keep thanking Him.

As you move into prayer and thanksgiving today, start by thanking Him for His glory providing your every need. Don't try to imagine how He will do it. To do that actually destroys faith. Just simply thank Him and leave the how to Him. He has the best 'how, what and when'!

ACTIVATION

Bring your need(s) to the throne of grace.

- A practical way to visualise bringing your need to His throne of grace is to first write the need on a piece of paper. Then take the paper with the need(s) and place it in your left hand and raise it before the Father. Then place His Word and pray over it with thanksgiving.

- Alternatively, ask Him to show you a different, yet creative and tangible way, to bring your need to Him.
- Keep a diary: write down the need, the date, and promises the Lord gives you. When the need and prayer is answered; again record the answer and the date it occurred. This will build your faith, help you to remember His miracles, and add fuel for giving thanks.

PRAYER

Praise Him for His glory.

Thank Him for meeting all your needs you have lifted up to Him according to His riches in glory.

If the need is financial; give thanks He owns the gold and silver, it is not too difficult for Him.

If your need is relationship or divine appointment—give thanks He is Lord of time and space.

If the answer to your need does not exist yet, He is the great Creator! He made the universe. Is your need harder to create than that? He has authority over death and can resurrect things.

Give thanks to God for the need you have for which He will get the glory.

Thank Him for providing the perfect answer.

BONUS DAY 41

Devil Defeated!

'The reason the Son of God was revealed was to undo and destroy the works of the devil.' (1 John 3:8 TPT)

'Then Jesus made a public spectacle of all the powers and principalities of darkness, stripping away from them every weapon and all their spiritual authority and power [governments and authority] to accuse us. And by the power of the cross, Jesus led them around as prisoners in a procession of triumph.' (Colossians 2:15 TPT)

'Let everyone give all their praise and thanks to the Lord! Here's why—he's better than anyone could ever imagine. Yes, he's always loving and kind, and his faithful love never ends. So, go ahead—let everyone know it! Tell the world how he broke through and delivered you from the power of darkness and has gathered us together from all over the world. He has set us free to be his very own!' (Psalm 107:1–3 TPT)

These are among my favourite Scriptures. What are your favourites?[102]

I love to thank Yeshua for coming to earth to destroy every work of the devil. And when I am faced with circumstances created by the devil's darkness, I love to remind the devil: Jesus came to earth in the flesh, He is the true light and He came to destroy every work of darkness.

When Yeshua overthrew the devil, He disempowered the worst despot in history! As an artistic person, I would love to see a dramatic enactment of Colossians 2 when Yeshua stripped the devil of all his weapons and all his power. Just imagine the script; 'Drop your weapons!' And to be a witness to the victory parade when Yeshua led the demonic hordes as His prisoners of war!

The devil thought he had won—BUT Jesus had a checkmate—He rose from the dead. Death could not hold Him. He overcame death, even through death!

In the last century we have witnessed many dictators on the earth. When they are deposed, overrun and driven from office there is such relief by the suffering populations. Unfortunately, in recent years, we have seen some dictators replaced by even worse despots. There is an important lesson to learn here. If we do not fill the vacuum created by a removed tyrant, it is filled by worse. Jesus spoke of a house being cleansed, but if it's not filled with the goodness and glory of God with the power of Holy Spirit, the demon will come back with seven more friends.

When Yeshua removes the devil's power—we God's people must first fill that space with the praises of God. We don't just have a victory gathering because the enemy was removed, but even more we must applaud and exalt the Name above all names. We magnify the Lord whose power, kingdom and authority is far above that of the enemy. But we must not do it just once. We must

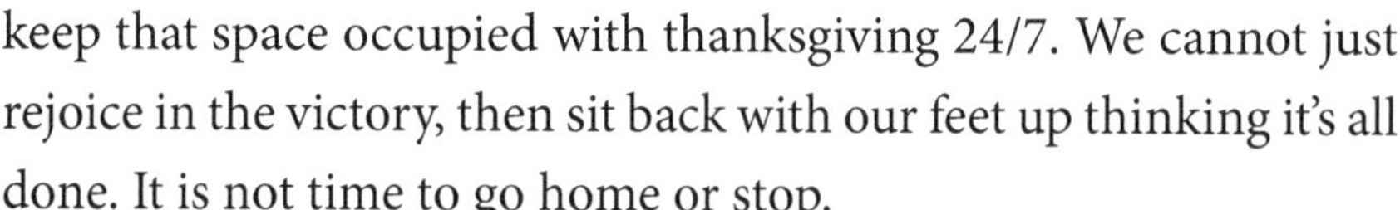

keep that space occupied with thanksgiving 24/7. We cannot just rejoice in the victory, then sit back with our feet up thinking it's all done. It is not time to go home or stop.

On earth today we must reinforce the victory Yeshua won. Every time we give thanks and praise Him in the face of our adversities, we are enforcing His victory. We enforce His victory as we develop a habitual lifestyle of praise and worship. We enforce the victory and authority of Yeshua every time we proclaim His name and demonstrate His love. We enforce His victory as we discover the fullness of offering the sacrifice of praise.

We stay in victory by giving thanks for what Yeshua did at the cross. We stay in victory as we lift His name above our challenging circumstances. We stay in victory when we give thanks in the midst of situations our flesh would prefer to grumble about. We stay in victory as we remind ourselves, and the devil, that Yeshua prevailed; the devil lost all his weapons and all his power.

If we get into grumbling, we give ground back to the devil. If we grumble and whinge, it is an invitation for those demons to return. When we grumble, we are offering the devil some of his ammunition back to use against us again! We are in effect doubting what Jesus did. 'Maybe only some of the devil's power was dismantled?'

We must agree with the apostles and with the Psalmist: 'Tell the world how He [Yeshua] broke through and delivered you from the power of darkness… He has set us free to be His very own!'(Psalm 107:1-3 TPT)

ACTIVATION

- Use today's Scriptures to give thanks to God.
- Lift before the Lord the circumstances where the devil is tormenting you and trying to convince you that you are defeated.
- Use today's Scriptures to remind the devil what Yeshua did.
- Repent of any times you have doubted the devil's power has been removed from your life.
- Use today's Scriptures to remind yourself what Yeshua did for you.
- Decree His Word over your situation today.

PRAYER

Loving and gracious Father, the Holy One of Israel, thank You for sending Your only Son to show us Your glory and to strip the devil of all his weapons, power and authority. I bless Yeshua who overcame death and hell—even from the grave! I thank You, Yeshua, for all You did to remove the devil's authority and power from my life and the lives of my loved ones! Amen

Continue praising Yeshua for what He achieved at the cross. Continue praising Him.

102. Appendix 1 has a list of Scriptures to help you habitually give thanks. You can add some of your favourites to that list.

BONUS DAY 42

You Are a Conqueror!

'Yet even in the midst of all these things, we triumph over them all, for God has made us to be more than conquerors, and His demonstrated love is our glorious victory over every-thing.' (Romans 8:37 TPT)

Begin today by personalising this Scripture into a prayer:

Righteous and Holy Father, I bless You. Even in the midst of all my circumstances, I am able to triumph. Through the love and power of Yeshua, You have made me to be a conqueror. (Name, lift to Him and thank Him for your impossible situations because He has enabled you to conquer______________.) Not only can I overcome any foe, but through Your love and Your demonstrated victory, I have access to that same victory. Your victory is my victory. Your resurrection is my resurrection. In Yeshua, I am more than a conqueror—above and beyond, to conquer every foe! Amen.

When we are slap bang in the middle of stuff, that is exactly the place we are to conquer. Jesus overcame principalities and powers in it—i.e. He conquered death in the midst of death. [103]

In 2018, Hurricane Michael devastated Florida. Images of the aftermath were extraordinary. So many destroyed homes. The most graphic images were the ones where the only thing left was concrete foundations.

The storms of life can create similar havoc. Those hurricane pictures were a reminder of the need to have solid spiritual foundations on Yeshua.

In the midst of life's trials we can feel discouraged and wonder if we will survive another gust of wind. We may even be tempted to let go and succumb to the winds of defeat. When life threatens our health, finances, relationships, confidence, and even our faith, do we get blown away or stay holding onto the Rock, the Messiah Yeshua?

Paul encourages us that we can triumph even in the midst of the storm. Being a conqueror is not about avoiding storms. Being a conqueror is surviving the storm and when the wind subsides, you are found to be still secured to the rock! If we remain holding on to Him, then it is a victory.

The Greek word used for conqueror is 'hupernikao' and means to gain a decisive victory. It is not just surviving, but to prevail means we also plunder the enemy! In a court of law, it would be the equivalent of first winning the case and then going on to get a huge payout as well. In war, it is not just to defeat the opposing army—but to possess new land.

The devil thought he had won when Jesus died on the cross. But in that storm, Jesus turned the situation around. Death could not hold Him! He overcame, defeated and conquered death and hell. It is that victory we have access to. Psalm 40:2,3 is a powerful prophetic reminder.

> *'He stooped down to lift me out of danger from the desolate pit I was in, out of the muddy mess I had fallen into. Now he's lifted me up into a firm, secure place and steadied me while I walk along his ascending path. A new song for a new day rises up in me every time I think about how he breaks through for me! Ecstatic praise pours out of my mouth until everyone hears how God has set me free.' (Psalm 40:2-3 TPT)*

Friends in New Zealand taught me a clever ditty for this Scripture:

'He took me out of the mire and set me in the choir.'

He places a new song in our heart. Thank Him for the song and for lifting you out of the mire. He is the glory and the lifter of your head. Thank the Lord; His love and power are lifting you from defeat to victory. Thank Him today; you not only conquer the enemy, but you get to plunder him as well!

Rejoice, your worship really touches the heart of God.

Rejoice, God has made you to be a conqueror. Rejoice, for in Him, you are a champion!

ACTIVATION

Today, what do you need to conquer? Are you faced with circumstances like the Churches in Revelation 2-3?

As you lift up your circumstances today, consider the reward given to the overcomers in Revelation. Let it encourage you to press into victory.

Those who overcome:

1. The ***loveless church*** gets to eat from the tree of life. (Revelation 2:7)
2. The ***persecuted church*** receives the crown of life and shall not be hurt by the second death. (Revelation 2:10, 11)
3. The ***compromising church*** will receive hidden manna to eat and a white stone, and on the stone a new name written. (Revelation 2:17) [104]
4. The ***corrupt church*** will be given power over the nations! (Revelation 2:26)
5. ***The dead church*** will be 'clothed in white garments', and Yeshua will speak their names before the Father and His angels. (Revelation 3:5)
6. And remain in the ***faithful church*** will be pillars in the temple of God, and they will have His name written on them. (Revelation 3:12)
7. The ***lukewarm church*** will be granted to sit with Yeshua on His throne. (Revelation 3: 21)

PRAYER

Almighty God, Holy One of Israel, Everlasting Father, Prince of Peace, I thank You for the demonstration of love and victory by Yeshua at the cross. It looked like defeat. But Your glory and Your Spirit enabled Him to overcome death. He triumphed in the midst of it. Where my circumstances look hopeless, I thank You for your victory.

I Praise You; Jesus demonstrated love one earth. He demonstrated love even as He faced unjust accusations, shame, torture, sorrow, death and hell. His demonstrated love is my victory over every situation today.

I Praise You, Yeshua; regardless of what I face, Your love and power enable me to be a conqueror. Amen

Keep praising Him—His love is penetrating your circumstances.

103 . "Having disarmed principalities and powers, He made a public spectacle of them, triumphing over them in it." Colossians 2: 15 (NKJV)

104. What is the 'white stone'? In the notes on this passage in The Passion Translation, it suggests a few possibilities. Any of these are possible for those who have overcome compromise.

1.The breastplate of the High priest contained different coloured stones. Each stone was engraved with the name of the tribe. Thus the High priest would bring the tribes before the Lord in intercession.

2. An acquittal in a court case (Acts 26:10)

3. Like the coal from the altar that purged the lips of Isaiah.

Appendices

APPENDIX 1

Praise Scriptures

Scriptures to Inspire Praise

Use this appendix as a starting point—add your own favourite inspirational Scriptures to encourage praise.

Psalm 100:2-4 (NKJV) 'Come before His presence with singing. Know that the Lord, He is God; It is He who has made us, and not we ourselves…Enter into His gates with thanksgiving, And into His courts with praise. Be thankful to Him, and bless His name.'

Psalm 136:1-4 (NKJV) 'Oh, give thanks to the Lord, for He is good! For His mercy endures forever. Oh, give thanks to the God of gods! For His mercy endures forever. Oh, give thanks to the Lord of lords! For His mercy endures forever: To Him who alone does great wonders, For His mercy endures forever…'

Psalm 119:164 (NKJV) 'Seven times a day I praise You, Because of Your righteous judgments.'

Psalm 18:48-49 (NKJV) 'He delivers me from my enemies. You also lift me up above those who rise against me; You have delivered me from the violent man. Therefore I will give thanks to You, O Lord, among the Gentiles, And sing praises to Your name.'

Psalm 139:1-2, 13-18 (TPT)' Lord, You know everything there is to know about me. You perceive every movement of my heart and soul, and You understand my every thought before it even enters my mind… You formed my innermost being, shaping my delicate inside and my intricate outside, and wove them all together in my mother's womb. I thank You, God, for making me so mysteriously complex! Everything You do is marvellously breathtaking…You even formed every bone in my body when You created me in the secret place, carefully, skilfully shaping me from nothing to something. You saw who You created me to be before I became me! Before I'd ever seen the light of day, the number of days You planned for me were already recorded in your book. Every single moment You are thinking of me! How precious and wonderful to consider that You cherish me constantly in your every thought!'

Psalm 149:3, 5-7 (NKJV) 'Praise His name with the dance; Let them sing praises to Him with the timbrel and harp… Let the saints be joyful in glory; Let them sing aloud on their beds. Let the high praises of God be in their mouth, And a two-edged sword in their hand, To execute vengeance on the nations, And punishments on the peoples…'

Jeremiah 32:17 (NKJV) 'Ah, Lord God! Behold, You have made the heavens and the earth by Your great power and outstretched arm. There is nothing too hard for You.'

Isaiah 58:9 (NKJV) 'Then you shall call, and the Lord will answer; You shall cry, and He will say, 'Here I am.' 'If you take away the yoke from your midst, The pointing of the finger, and speaking wickedness…'

1 Thessalonians 5:16-18 (NKJV) 'Rejoice always, pray without ceasing, in everything give thanks; for this is the will of God in Christ Jesus for you.'

Revelation 11:16-17 (NKJV) 'And the twenty-four elders who sat before God on their thrones fell on their faces and worshiped

God, saying: 'We give You thanks, O Lord God Almighty, The One who is and who was and who is to come, Because You have taken Your great power and reigned.'

Romans 8:28, 31, 37-39 (NKJV) 'And we know that all things work together for good to those who love God, to those who are the called according to His purpose. What then shall we say to these things? If God is for us, who can be against us? Yet in all these things we are more than conquerors through Him who loved us. For I am persuaded that neither death nor life, nor angels nor principalities nor powers, nor things present nor things to come, nor height nor depth, nor any other created thing, shall be able to separate us from the love of God which is in Christ Jesus our Lord.'

Colossians 2:12-15 (NKJV) '…God, who raised Him from the dead. And you, being dead in your trespasses and the un-circumcision of your flesh, He has made alive together with Him, having forgiven you all trespasses, having wiped out the handwriting of requirements that was against us, which was contrary to us. And He has taken it out of the way, having nailed it to the cross. Having disarmed principalities and powers, He made a public spectacle of them, triumphing over them in it.'

1 John 3:8b (NKJV) 'For this purpose the Son of God was manifested, that He might destroy the works of the devil.'

1 John 4:4 (NKJV) 'You are of God, little children, and have overcome them, because He who is in you is greater than he who is in the world.'

Romans 4:17b (NKJV) '...God, who gives life to the dead and calls those things which do not exist as though they did…'

APPENDIX 2

Sample Praise Prayer

- **Spend a few moments to thank and praise the Lord. Use your mother tongue or heavenly language.**
- **This prayer is a suggested way to personalise Scripture.**

Lord God Almighty, You are the Creator of the Universe. By Your great strength and power, You made all things. Nothing in my life is too difficult for you![105] You are greater, bigger and more powerful than every challenging circumstance in my life. I now lift these up to You_______________

(Praise Him!)

I am so grateful You turn around every situation for good. What the enemy means for evil, You re-create and making something good and beautiful. You are sovereignly making every crooked place become straight! I thank You, Lord, for every circumstance in my life right now. I thank You for every person You have placed in my life. I thank You that Your goodness and mercy follow me every day. Thank-you for Your love, joy, peace, patience, kindness, goodness, faithfulness, gentleness and self-control. Thank-you that the fruit of Your Spirit is growing in me.[106]

(Praise Him!)

You have given me every resource from heaven to help me through every situation and to overcome! Your extravagant love keeps flowing into me until I am filled to overflowing with Your goodness. Your supernatural strength floods my innermost being with Your divine might and explosive power. You forgive my every failure. Every accusation against me is nailed to the cross. Yeshua, You came to earth to destroy every work of the devil. You disarmed every principality and power and stripped them of their power.[107]

(Praise Him!)

Yeshua, Your resurrection is mine. Now I am alive with You and You live in me. Like Abraham, I believe You give life to the dead and call into existence things that don't even exist. I call forth resurrection life into my circumstances and dreams. I thank-you for every promise You have given to me, and according to Your faithfulness and resurrection power I call those words into existence.[108]

(Praise Him!)

Heavenly Father, I thank You that Your grace is sufficient for me.

Greater is He who is in me than he who is in the world. If You are for me, who can be against me? Because I am hidden in Messiah, the devil cannot find me! You are empowering me supernaturally to survive and thrive each of these circumstances. Nothing: no trouble, distress, persecution, hunger, nakedness, danger, death or life, angels or rulers, anything present or in the future, forces or powers in the world above or in the world below, or anything else in creation, can separate me from Your endless love that is without measure![109]

(Praise Him!)

---

105. Jeremiah 32:17
106. Romans 8:28; Isaiah 40:4; Psalm 23:6; Galatians 5:22
107. Ephesians 1:3 (TPT); Ephesians 3:14-19 (TPT); Colossians 2:14
108. Colossians 3:1; Romans 4:17
109. 2 Corinthians 12:9; Romans 8:31-39

APPENDIX 3

Identify Your Grumble Habit

When loss and disappointment hit us—how do we respond? How do we process? Where do we go for comfort?

The answers to these questions will help us discover our grumbling habit. Grumbles especially occur when life does not go how we expect or desire. We tend to grumble when life appears unfair, impossible or extremely painful.

How do we process loss? How do we process real or perceived injustices? The fact is everyone needs time to process and to heal. But everyone processes differently. Some like to talk and talk and talk. Others like to be quiet and reflect. Others go into an unhelpful denial. Processing differences can be based on gender and personality differences. Reality is—we are all wired differently!

Our resilience will be impacted by our choice to praise or grumble. Our decision to praise or grumble will depend on three factors;

- Level of maturity and walk with God
- How we process loss
- How committed we are to press into the Lord.

Time does not heal all wounds. Psychologists, counsellors and pastors can help alleviate issues with understanding and strategies, but only Jesus can heal broken hearts. (Isaiah 61)

Honesty

However we process, honesty with God is vital. We can only enter into true gratitude when we honestly admit our reactions to life's disappointments, losses, frustrations, cares and wounds. We need to be brutally honest with the Lord about our anger, frustration, grief, and loss. Pretence and denial will not fix it.

Yet every person has a different route to healing. Seek His specific pathway for you. Digest His love and truth as you would eat a good meal—let them soak into your soul.

Gender Differences in Processing

Especially within a marriage, we have to realise that men and women do process differently. Understanding these differences helps us to empathise and support loved ones.

Let me illustrate the difference between the way men and women process stuff through the example of a set of Christmas lights.

When a severe crisis occurs, a woman will discover all her lights will go out. A woman's emotions, thoughts and decisions are all inter-wired and in a crisis her circuits go down. She will not be able to function properly.

However, a man in the same situation will respond differently. Men are wired differently. A man, in a similar crisis to the lady, will appear to just lose one light of the whole set and thus able to keep functioning. It is like he can put the crisis into a room and lock the door, appear to forget it and deal with the crisis apparently unaffected.

People often comment that women are more sensitive to the Holy Spirit. The above scenarios show that a woman's thoughts and emotions are all inter-wired. If a woman is open to the Lord, she will seek healing as a priority. She can't function with lights out and knows only the Lord can fix her problem. Hence, women are more likely to seek help than men.

The way a man is wired is helpful during a crisis. He is able to get his family to safety. He is able to resolve or work through the crisis to get some sense of resolution. The problem is after the crisis is over.

Ideally, a man would go back and fix the broken globe. But this ideal is where the world and the Church have not helped men. The rest of the lights work, so we say to men; 'Don't worry about the one broken globe! Get on with life.' So many men leave the locked room bolted and continue on with life. Or at least try to.

The problem is, the locked room of the soul continues to hurt and fester. Then the next crisis comes and causes another globe to go, and then another. The soul wounds unknowingly build until all their lights are out. Sadly, if men wait until then to process their disappointments, they have often forgotten what is inside all these locked rooms. Or if they do open them, they are overwhelmed and don't know where to start. They may have forgotten what caused the problem in the first place! Denial and ignoring issues increase and increase until there is a serious crisis.

Male or female, crisis affect us all, and we need the healing power of the Lord. Anne Hamilton asks the important question: when disappointment hits us, where do we go?[110]

Do we go to the Lord or do we get comfort elsewhere? If we go to the Lord for help, we will end up in praise. If we go elsewhere for comfort, we will be open to grumbling and demonic attack.

If you want to explore these areas of healing;

1. Consider the following ways that people process and consider where you fit.
2. Read Anne Hamilton's book Hidden in the Cleft: True and False refuges[111]
3. Seek the Holy Spirit for healing and prayer ministry.

Identify Three Serious Grumbling Processes[112]

1. **Vent-ors**—they don't want a solution, they just need to get the issue off their chest. They will talk and talk and talk. They just want your ear!

2. **Sympathy seekers**—are definitely worse off than everyone else and need your sympathy—they love pity-parties.

3. **Chronic grumbler**—constant complaining has become such a habit and a stronghold of thinking, perhaps they are not even aware they complain.

Grumbling can disrupt our ability to process the difficulties in life accurately.

Healing of deep issues will take more than 40 days of fasting from grumbling. However, it will position your heart to receive His answers, His love, His direction and His resolutions.

If you need to do as I did, when you finish one 40 day fast, start another. And keep doing it until you experience breakthrough!

And for serious issues, do seek professional help. (Please Note: If gratitude and praise do not shift any serious foreboding, deep seated fears, anxieties or issues; you may need to seek the help of a prayer counselor, deliverance ministry, or Christian psychologist or other suitable professional to help you through.) Ask the Lord to show you, and to find, the right person for you.

---

110. Anne Hamilton. Hidden in the Cleft: True and False Refuges. Strategies of the Threshold, #4. QLD, Australia: Armour Books, 2019.

111. Ibid.

112. Three Types of Complaining https://www.psychologytoday.com/au/blog/significant-results/201706/the-three-types-complaining

APPENDIX 4

Leviathan & Jezebel Checklist

LEVIATHAN

Job 3:8; Job 41; Psalm 74:4; Psalm 104:26; Isaiah 27:1

Manifestations

- Described as a twisted serpent, dragon, crocodile, king of Egypt
- King of Pride
- Resists Holy Spirit
- Twisted communications (The crocodile has a big mouth! Its mouth is 2/3rds of its body and has 30 teeth each side!)
- Activated by dishonour
- Backlash, revenge, whiplash (tail)
- Death and destruction

Overcome by

- Stay out of its habitat (Mouth = watch communications. Tail = backlash)

- The Lord is the only one who can kill it - with His sword.

  Jesus is the dragon slayer.
- By the blood of the Lamb, word of testimony and surrender of life. (Revelation 12:7-12)

JEZEBEL

1 Kings 16-19, 21; 2 Kings 9; Revelation 2:20

Manifestations

- Idolatry – Baal worship
- Illegitimate power, take-over
- Immorality
- Seduction
- Murder of innocents – sacrifice of firstborn to Baal, abortion
- Kills true prophets and prophetic.
  Feeds and promotes false prophets.
- Destroys the altars of the Lord

Overcome by

- Thanksgiving and praise release joy.

  The joy of the Lord is your strength to overcome these attacks.
- Stop tolerating her works
- Prophetic and kingly decrees enable those who have been emotionally and spiritually castrated by her to summon their strength in God and push her out of the window.
- The hound dogs of heaven

APPENDIX 5

Born Again – Redeemed

In the first paragraphs of Day 1 '*Gratitude is a Password*', I used two terms that are common in the Bible: 'born again', and 'redeemed'.

> "In this age of computers and cyberspace, we all need passwords. We need them to access emails, online banking, online shopping, and programs like Google, YouTube and the like. Everyone needs a password to get access. First you must sign up. Then you select a password, and each time you return, you enter the password and voila, you are in. Our 'password' to the Presence of the Lord is praise and gratitude...We 'sign up' when we are ***born again, redeemed*** and cleansed by the blood of Jesus. Without that sign-up, our password is not recognised. Signing up is usually a one-time event."

If you are reading and doing this "*Grumble Fast*" yet uncertain of the meaning of the terms, 'born again' and 'redeemed', or if you are unsure if you have actually 'signed up', then this appendix is for you. It's also a great reference tool.

Born Again

In John 3:3-8 Jesus had a conversation with Nicodemus who was perplexed at the miracles Jesus was performing. The answer Jesus gave was disconcerting to this Jewish lawyer.

> *'Most assuredly, I say to you, unless one is born again, he cannot see the kingdom of God.'*

Nicodemus struggled with this idea because his thinking was limited to natural birth. His follow-up question revealed a weird scenario in his imagination: trying to re-enter his mother's womb for a second time! Jesus gave further explanation.

> *'Most assuredly, I say to you, unless one is born of water and the Spirit, he cannot enter the kingdom of God.6 That which is born of the flesh is flesh, and that which is born of the Spirit is spirit.'*

Mankind has a body, soul and spirit. 'Born again' is a phrase which speaks of a new nature within our *spirit* rather than getting a new body. God is a spirit and our fellowship with Him is spirit to spirit. A spiritual new birth is obtained with the help of the Holy Spirit and by activating faith in Jesus.

God Loves You

We are wired for love. Yet Jesus was requiring a change of nature in our spirit. Was God criticizing the way we were? Jesus knew that Nicodemus (and us) would subconsciously be wondering about God's motivation. Jesus (and later Paul) assures the motivation for God to connect with man, is His deep, deep love.

> **John 3:16** – *'For God so loved the world that He gave His only begotten Son, that whoever believes in Him should not perish but have everlasting life.'*

> **Romans 5:8** – *'But God demonstrates His own love toward us, in that while we were still sinners, Christ died for us.'*

All Are Sinners

A new nature is based on the Biblical premise that all of mankind, without exception, is born in the image of God but that image was corrupted, degraded, and despoiled by sin.

> **Romans 3:23** –*'All have **sinned** and fall short of the glory of God.'*

The word 'sin' is an archery term and means to 'miss the mark'. The flaw in human flesh means, even if we want to, we are unable to attain the 'glory of God. Thus we 'fall short'.

God's Remedy: Redeemed by the Blood of Jesus

Though created in the image of God, Satan subverted, deceived and stole the souls of mankind. Our natural inclination became bent to rebel against The Creator. Hence, we became citizens of the kingdom of darkness and death. And generation after generation, we inherit and pass on this rebellious sin nature. But there are no rebels in heaven!

God wanted us back under His loving care. He wanted us back as citizens of heaven. His remedy? Redemption. To redeem something is to liberate, deliver, even, 'buy back'. The price paid to legally buy us back was the blood of Jesus, which poured out when He died on the cross.

> **1 Peter 1:18** – *'You were not redeemed with corruptible things, **like** silver or gold … [19] but with the precious blood of Christ, as of a lamb without blemish.'*

> **Revelation 1:5 (GW)** – *'Glory and power forever and ever belong to the one [Jesus] who loves us and has freed us from our sins by His blood.'*

Revelation 5:9 [Lamb of God] – *'You were slain and have redeemed us to God by Your blood.'*

The blood of Jesus is powerful to redeem or buy us back so we belong to God. His blood also releases forgiveness for our rebellion. And His blood delivers, cleanses, and heals our soul from the damage inflicted by the devil. The blood of Jesus brings freedom from the guilt and shame of sin.

Access God's Gift

We access God's gift of eternal life by believing in Jesus. Under the law, rebellion was punishable by death. Though we are all born rebels, Jesus was born perfect and sinless. He chose to be our substitute, and lovingly paid our penalty of a rebellious son.

All we have to do is acknowledge we are rebels, accept Jesus is the Son of the Living God and receive His free gift. Too simple? Maybe. But it's not easy to admit we are rebels. It takes real courage, and humility, to admit we are fundamentally flawed and need a saviour who is greater than us!

Romans 6:23 – *'For the wages of sin is death, but the gift of God is **eternal life** in Christ Jesus our Lord.'*

1 Corinthians *15:3,4 – 'Christ died for our sins according to the Scriptures, [4]and that He was buried, and that He rose again the third day according to the Scriptures.'*

How to 'Sign Up'

The answer is found in Romans 10: 9, 13 which says:

*'If you confess with your mouth the Lord Jesus and believe in your heart that God has raised Him from the dead, **you will be saved**... [13]whoever calls on the name of the Lord **shall** be saved.'*

1. Acknowledge you are a rebel who needs redemption.

2. Call on the name of the Lord to be delivered.

3. Believe in your heart (not just your head) that Jesus is the Son of God, He loves you, He died for you, He rose from the dead and His blood can now deliver and cleanse you from sin.

4. Speak those beliefs out with your mouth, and preferably, before two or three witnesses.

Are you ready to 'sign up'? Here is a prayer to assist you. Also, to help you 'remember' the moment, I encourage you to read and then speak the prayer, sign and date your confession before a witness.

> "I confess I am sinner who has rebelled against God. I have fallen short of His great glory. I believe Jesus is the Son of God who came to earth in human flesh and died for my sins on the cross. His resurrection conquered sin and death to give me new life. I call on the name of Jesus to save and deliver me from my sin nature. According to Scripture, Jesus is faithful to forgive me, and the blood of Jesus frees me from sin and cleanses my conscience from the useless things I have done. Now I am free to serve and worship the living God!"

Name____

Date____

Witness ______________________________________

Status of Witness (Relative, Friend, Pastor, Neighbor etc.)

____

Bibliography

Brown, Michael L. PhD. *Jezebel's War with America.* Florida, USA: Charisma Media /Charisma House Book Group, 2019.

Freed, Sandie. *The Jezebel Yoke.* Chosen - a division of Baker Publishing Group, 2012.

Hamilton, Anne. *Dealing with Python. Strategies of the Threshold, #1.* QLD, Australia: Armour Books, 2017.

Hamilton, Anne. Dealing with ZIZ: *Spirit of Forgetting. Strategies of the Threshold, #2.* Armour Books, 2018.

Hamilton, Anne. *Hidden in the Cleft:* True and False Refuge. Strategies of the Threshold, #4. QLD, Australia: Armour Books, 2019.

Hamilton, Anne. 'Rejection 1 & 2.' YouTube. Tabernacle of David - Bendigo, 2019.
https://www.youtube.com/watch?v=sDhH80tJVQE&t=1s.

Jackson, John Paul. *Unmasking the Spirit of Jezebel.* Streams Publishing, 2002.

Joyner, Rick. *Fire on the Mountain; Book Two, The Valley.* 2 vols. *Fire on the Mountain.* Morningstar Publications, 2018.

LeClaire, Jennifer. *Defeating Jezebel.* USA: Chosen, a division of Baker Publishing Group, 2013.

LeClaire, Jennifer. *Jezebel's Puppets.* Charisma House, 2016. www.jenniferleclsaire.org.

Webb, Ruth. *Restoring True Worship.* Heart of the Psalmist Inc, 1993. www.tabernacleofdavid.org.au

Worship Resources

BOOK by Ruth Webb

Restoring True Worship: Music, Holiness & Revival

© 1993 (350 page paperback)

https://www.tabernacleofdavid.org.au/shop/book-32.html

A wealth of information about God's intention for music. In this book, Ruth Webb provides an overview of the battle for true worship against idolatry and demonic intrusion, especially through cultural temptations to the Church. Ruth also provides guidelines to discern godly music and shows the links between pure music in worship, the restoration of the Tabernacle of David and revival fires.

RECORDED (DVD) TEACHINGS by Ruth Webb

- **Transformed by Love**
- **Church Transition: Institution to Bride**
- **Shofars and Banners**
- **Frequencies of the Glory**
- **Spirit of Rock**

https://www.tabernacleofdavid.org.au/shop/dvd-teaching-31.html

INSTRUMENTAL MUSIC by Ruth Webb

Available as Digital Download or CD

https://www.tabernacleofdavid.org.au/shop/cd-29.html

INSTRUMENTAL: piano (Ruth Webb), violin (Prody G), orchestra

- **Be Still**
- **Gardens of Love**

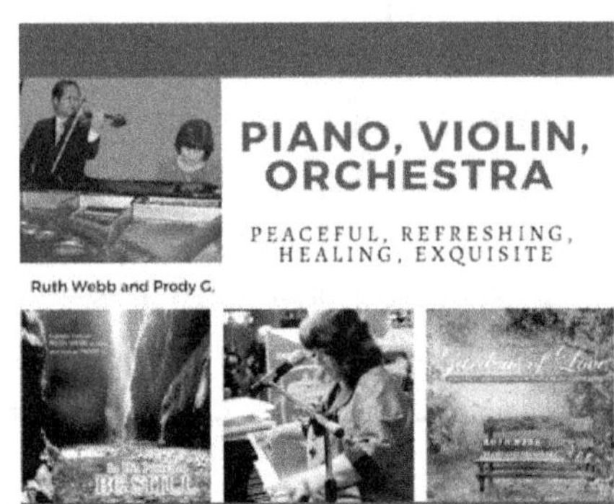

LIVE PROPHETIC WORSHIP: Tabernacle of David worship team, Ruth Webb worship leader and psalmist, plus instrumentals: piano, violin, drums, percussion and orchestra

- **Holy One**
- **Welcome King of Glory** (3 Albums in one package!)
  Album One: High Praise
  Album Two: Intimate worship
  Album Three: Decrees in prophetic song

About the Author

RUTH WEBB is co-founder of Heart of the Psalmist, Inc. (worship resources) with her husband Laurence. A decade later they pioneered Tabernacle of David (Bendigo). T.O.D is a centre for Throne-Room Worship where Ruth teaches, equips and facilitates space for worship-warriors.

Ruth received the Lord's call to worship ministry at just age 11. In response, she developed her musical skills and dedicated her gift to exalt the Lord. Ruth graduated from Melbourne University with a Bachelor of Music Education (piano and composition), and initially worked as a secondary school music teacher and adjudicator.

Ruth has a passion to see ***every*** believer ***engaged*** in intimate worship, reflecting the pure and powerful sounds of heaven. Ruth's expertise and gifting are well recognised as evidenced by numerous invitations to serve congregations, prayer houses and ministries both across Australia and internationally.

She has released seven worship albums and this is her second major writing. For more information, to access resources or to make contact, go to: www.tabernacleofdavid.org.au

www.ingramcontent.com/pod-product-compliance
Lightning Source LLC
Chambersburg PA
CBHW050630300426
44112CB00012B/1731

* 9 7 8 0 9 5 8 7 4 3 7 3 0 *